IT Governance

A Pocket Guide

based on

CobiT®

IT Governance

A Pocket Guide

based on COBIT®

ITSM Pocket Library

COLOPHON

Title: IT Governance - A Pocket Guide, based on COBIT®

Authors: Koen Brand & Harry Boonen

Chief editor: Jan van Bon (Inform-IT, *editors & innovators*, the Netherlands)

International Review Team:
Rolf Akker, BHVB, the Netherlands (*previewer*)
Menno Arentsen, Ernst & Young EDP Audit, the Netherlands (*previewer*)
Raoul Assaf, ARTUTA, Argentina
David Aveiro, Organizational Engineering Center, Portugal
Gustav van den Berg, UWV, the Netherlands (*previewer*)
Pierre Bernard, Pink Elephant, Canada
David Bingham, Fujitsu Consulting, UK
Michael Böcker, Serima Consulting GmbH, Germany
József Borda, CISA, Hunaudit Ltd., Hungary
Maarten Bordewijk, PinkRoccade Educational Services, the Netherlands
Gerard Brantjes, Brantjes Advies Buro, the Netherlands
Luigi Buglione, École de Technologie Supérieure (ETS) - Université du Québec, Canada
Jeff Carter PMP, MSFmentor, USA
Marien de Clercq, University Centre for Information Technology - University of Nijmegen,
    the Netherlands
Rod Crowder, OpsCentre, Australia
Dr Brian Cusack, Auckland University of Technology, New Zealand
Kim Delgadillo, IBM Business Consulting Services, Belgium
Helga Dohle, exagon consulting & solutions gmbh, Germany
Ton Dohmen, PriceWaterhouseCoopers, the Netherlands (*previewer*)
Troy DuMoulin, Pink Elephant International, Canada
Isaac Eliahou, AtosOrigin, the Netherlands (*previewer*)
Martin Erb, USA
Péter Füzi, Salix Informatikai Bt, Hungary
Wolfgang Goltsche, Siemens Business Services, Germany
Vincent Haenecour, Consultis, Belgium
Oscar Halfhide, LogicaCMG, the Netherlands
Franz J. Hareter, Skybow AG, Switzerland
Hussein Hassanali Haji, Sidat Hyder Morshed Associates (Pvt.) Ltd., Pakistan
Peter Hill, Info Sec Africa, South Africa
Ton van den Hoogen, Tot Z BV, the Netherlands
Göran Jonsson, Sweden
Jörn Kettler, Serima Consulting GmbH, Germany
Sergei Konakov, 5-55, Russia
Ben Kooistra, Capgemini, the Netherlands

Nicolay Krachun, Motorola GSG, Russia

Emmanuel Lagouvardos, CISA, Emporiki Bank, Greece

Alexandre Levinson, Tolkin, France

Peiwei Lu, SinoServiceOne Ltd, P.R.China

Steve Mann, SM2 Ltd, UK

Luis F. Martínez, Abast Systems, Spain

Jos Mertens, PlanIT, Belgium

Cees Michielsen, Océ-Technologies BV, the Netherlands

Peter Musgrave, Reccan Ltd, UK

Fred van Noord, GvIB Society for Information Security professionals, the Netherlands

Peter Palatinus, Hewlett-Packard GmbH, Germany

Michael Parkinson, KPMG, Australia

Antonio de Pastors, Synstar Computer Services, Spain

Vladimir Pavlov, eLine Software Inc., Ukraine

Gert van der Pijl, Erasmus University/Eurac, the Netherlands (*previewer*)

Karel van der Poel, Mirror42, the Netherlands (*previewer*)

Gerrit Post, the Netherlands (*previewer*)

Michael Pototsky, IT Expert, Russia

Sylvie Prime Van Parys, CRP Henri Tudor, Luxembourg

Ferran Puentes, Abast Systems, Spain

Max Shanahan, Max Shanahan & Associates, Australia

Andie Shih, ITIL International Examination Agency - North America

Ron Sintemaartensdijk, Sogeti Nederland, the Netherlands

Helen A. Sotiriou CISA, Emporiki Bank, Greece

Peter Spermon RE RI CISA, Inspectie Werk & Inkomen (IWI), the Netherlands

Rainer Sponholz, Ernst & Young AG, Germany

Heather Stebbings MSc. DMS, CSTC Consulting, UK

Fred Steenwinkel, VRO/IIA, the Netherlands (*previewer*)

Philip Stubbs, Sheridan Insititute of Technology and Advanced Learning, Canada

Ruedi Stucki, Zurich Financial Services, Switzerland

Maxim Taradin, JSC Vimpelcom (Beeline™), Russia

Karin Thelemann, Ernst & Young AG, Germany

Sascha Thies, exagon consulting & solutions gmbh, Germany

Antonio Valle, Abast Systems, Spain

Wiley Vasquez, BMC Software, USA

Han Verniers, LogicaCMG ICT Management, the Netherlands (*previewer*)

Jurgen van der Vlugt, ABN AMRO Bank, the Netherlands

Clemens Willemsen, KIBO, the Netherlands (*previewer*)

Conn Wood, Foster-Melliar, South Africa

People marked with '(*previewer*)' are members of the core project team and contributed
to de design of this Pocket Guide

Publisher: Van Haren Publishing (info@vanharen.net)

ISBN: 90-77212-19-1

Editions: First impression, second edition, September 2004

Design & Layout: DTPresto Design & Layout, Zeewolde-NL

TRADEMARK NOTICE

CoBiT® is a registered trademark of ISACA/ITGI - Information Systems Audit and Control Association / IT Governance Institute®

ITIL® is a registered trademark of OGC - the Office of Government Commerce.

DISCLAIMER

Neither ISACA nor ITGI endorse, sponsor, or are otherwise affiliated with this publication and they do not warrant or guarantee its accuracy.

TABLE OF CONTENTS

FOREWORD

This IT Governance Pocket Guide is the result of a project that involved many experts from all over the world. It started out as a compact reference to one framework, but it grew into an original document on IT Governance, building on many pieces of knowledge from various sources, going back into the sources of these sources, and adding pieces to the puzzle.

The project started out in the Netherlands, where a dedicated preview team designed the initial structure of this guide. In the course of the project, a huge amount of material was made available by an international team of reviewers from all kinds of origin, ranging from highly experienced practitioners in the auditing business, to presidents of ISACA chapters and academics, and to skilled IT Service Management experts and trainers. The rare combination of knowledge that was collected, enabled the development of a new instrument that will fit both worlds: Auditing and IT Service Management. It will offer the auditors a bridge to the service management business - the new wave in IT - and it will offer the service management world its long desired next step: a management instrument that enables them to put the pieces of the puzzle together, get a clear picture, and get - and stay - *in control*.

And that is what we're after: to be in control. Not only because new rules force us to do so, but also because it will bring some meaning to all the effort that was spilled on the way getting here.

And although it definitely will not be 'the silver bullet', I do think this publication can bring us one big step ahead.

This guide is part of a project that will also produce a new infrastructure of training and certification facilities, as well as new initiatives in supporting software tools, and complementary guidance.

I sincerely hope you will enjoy the efforts of the team.

Any comments and suggestions regarding the content of this pocket guide are welcomed by the project team. Please mail to j.van.bon@inform-it.org

Jan van Bon,

chief editor

Introduction

This book provides an overview of IT Governance in a handy pocket guide format.

It is provided for two purposes. First, it is a quick-reference guide to IT Governance for people that are not acquainted with this field of work. Second, it is a high-level introduction to ITGI's[1] open standard 'CobiT' that will encourage further study. Please note that this guide follows the process structure of CobiT, since we found that to be best practice, but it differs from CobiT in several ways, adding new information to the structure, from the perspective of IT Service Management.

The pocket guide is aimed at Business and IT (Service) Managers, Consultants, Auditors and anyone interested in learning more about the possible application of IT Governance standards in the IT management domain. In addition, it provides students in IT and Business Administration with a compact reference to CobiT.

After an introduction to IT Governance and CobiT in general, you will find information about ITGI's CobiT publications, since we encourage the use of CobiT. In the next section, you will find a description of the 34 processes that were identified from many international standards. This Pocket Guide adds new information to the various sources that were used to describe IT Governance, including CobiT. Workflow diagrams and process models have been added as an extension to existing material. A full set of detailed descriptions will be made available in 'IT Governance - An Introduction', the training book that follows this pocket guide in 2004. The last part of the book provides some guidance on CobiT implementation and the relationship with other methods and frameworks.

1) The ITGI as a not-for-profit organization has made CobiT an Open Standard with the majority of documents available for free download from the Internet to encourage wide adoption, however reproduction of any of the CobiT content for commercial use is not permitted without the ITGI's prior consent.

Context

In a book about IT Governance it is sensible to analyse the position of IT Governance in relation to other governance frameworks. The most comprehensive framework encountered in literature is in a discussion paper by the Chartered Institute of Management Accountants (CIMA). In this paper Enterprise Governance is a term used to describe a framework that covers both the *Corporate Governance* and the *Business Governance* aspects of the organisation.

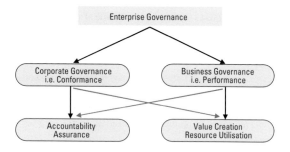

Figure 1.1 The Enterprise Governance framework (Source: CIMA)

CIMA uses the following definition of *Enterprise Governance*:

> *'Enterprise Governance is the set of responsibilities and practices exercised by the board and executive management with the goal of providing strategic direction, ensuring that objectives are achieved, ascertaining that risks are managed appropriately and verifying that the enterprise's resources are used responsibly (CIMA, referencing ISACF®).'*

According to CIMA there are two dimensions of Enterprise Governance: conformance and performance. In general, the conformance dimension is approached in the *ex post* (retrospective) view, while the performance dimension is approached in the *ex ante* (prospective) view.

The lines in figure 1.1 show that, although conformance feeds directly to accountability & assurance and performance to value creation & resource utilisation, conformance can also feed to value creation & resource utilisation while performance can feed to accountability & assurance.

Corporate Governance, as the conformance dimension of Enterprise Governance, has had significant coverage following the recent corporate scandals. In the wake of these scandals, which also included the demise of one of the Big Five accountancy firms, new regulations designed to strengthen Corporate Governance were introduced in the US, in Europe and in many other jurisdictions. In the US the Sarbanes-Oxley Act was introduced for this reason. In Europe the Winter Report issued recommendations to provide for a modern regulatory framework for company law to the European Commission.

Among its recommendations is that companies that are traded on open markets provide a coherent and descriptive statement covering the key elements of Corporate Governance rules and practices in their annual report and on their web site.

The Organisation of Economic Co-operation and Development (OECD) defines *Corporate Governance* in the following way:

> *Corporate Governance is the system by which business corporations are directed and controlled. The Corporate Governance structure specifies the distribution of rights and responsibilities among different participants in the corporation, such as the board, managers, shareholders and other stakeholders, and spells out the rules and procedures for*

making decisions on corporate affairs. By doing this, it also
provides the structure through which the company objec-
tives are set, and the means of attaining those objectives
and monitoring performance. (OECD)

The importance of good Corporate Governance is recognised
worldwide. It must lead to improved responsiveness to shareholder
interest by attempting to balance the CEO's power with the board's
ability to act as genuine custodians of the organisation.

Business Governance, as the performance dimension of Enterprise
Governance, focuses on the board's role in making strategic decisions, risk assessment and understanding the drivers for business
performance.

The attention to Corporate Governance also raises the question
whether the IT used for supporting business processes is adequately controlled. This leads to an increase in attention for IT
Governance in many organisations. Because IT is an integral part
of business operations, IT Governance is an integral ingredient of
Corporate Governance.

IT Governance has been defined in many different ways. In this
publication IT Governance is defined as follows:

IT Governance is the system by which IT within enterprises
is directed and controlled. The IT Governance structure
specifies the distribution of rights and responsibilities among
different participants, such as the board, business and IT
managers, and spells out the rules and procedures for ma-
king decisions on IT. By doing this, it also provides the struc-
ture through which the IT objectives are set, and the means
of attaining those objectives and monitoring performance.

Corporate Governance	Business Governance	IT Governance
Separation of ownership and control	Direction and control of the business	Direction and control of IT
Ex post	*Ex ante*	*Ex ante*
• Duties of Directors/ Leaders • Legislative/Fiduciary Compliance & Control • Shareholder Rights • Ethics & Integrity • Business Operations, Risks & Control • Financial Accounting & Reporting • Asset Management • Risk Management	• Business Goals & Objectives • Business Strategy & Planning • Business Activities & Processes • Innovation & Research Capabilities • Knowledge & Intellectual Capital • Information & its Management • Human Resources Management • Customer Service & Relationships • In- and External Communication • Performance Control	• IT Objectives • Alignment with Enterprise Objectives • IT Resources • Information Knowledge Management • IT Strategy & Planning • IT Acquisition & Implementation • IT Operations, Risks & Control • IT Asset Management • IT Risk Management

Table 1.1 Governance characteristics

Table 1.1, on the previous page, compares the most important characteristics of Corporate Governance, Business Governance and IT Governance within Enterprise Governance.

IT Governance ensures that IT is properly aligned with business processes and is properly organised and controlled. IT Governance provides the structure that links IT processes, IT resources and information to enterprise strategies and objectives.

IT Governance integrates and institutionalises best practices of planning, organising, acquiring, implementing, delivering, supporting, and monitoring IT performance, to ensure that the enterprise's information and related technology support its business objectives. IT Governance enables the enterprise to take full advantage of its information, thereby maximising benefits and capitalising on opportunities thus leveraging competitive advantage.

Sources for IT Governance

Regarding governance there are several sources that provide basic knowledge. In the following paragraphs some background on the major sources is presented.

COSO

In 1992, the Committee of Sponsoring Organizations of the Treadway Commission issued *'Internal Control - Integrated Framework'*. This publication established a framework for internal control and provided evaluation tools which business and other entities can use to evaluate their control systems (figure 1.2).

The framework identifies and describes five interrelated components necessary for effective internal control.

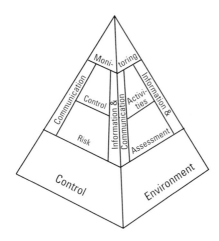

Figure 1.2 COSO Internal Control - Integrated Framework (Source COSO)

In *'Internal Control - Integrated Framework'*, COSO defined internal control as a process, effected by an entity's board of directors, management and other personnel, designed to provide reasonable assurance regarding the achievement of objectives in the following categories:

- Effectiveness and efficiency of operations
- Reliability of financial reporting
- Compliance with applicable laws and regulations.

In 2004 the COSO Enterprise Risk Management (ERM) is to be published. *Enterprise risk management* is broader than internal control, expanding and elaborating on internal control to form a more robust conceptualisation focusing more fully on risk. The enterprise risk management framework expands on the internal control framework as follows:

- Four categories of objectives are specified: *operations*, *reporting*, *compliance* and *strategic objectives*. Reporting now includes reports used internally by management and those issued to external parties. Strategic objectives have been added as a new category.
- ERM considers risk from a 'portfolio' perspective.
- The framework takes into consideration the amount of risk a company is willing to accept to achieve its goals.
- Events that can influence the company are identified. Those that can hold negative impact represent risks.
- Risk assessment is extended.
- ERM identifies four categories of risk response - *avoid*, *reduce*, *share* and *accept*. Responses are being considered both for individual risk effect and for aggregate effect.
- ERM expands on the information and communication component, considering data derived from past, present and potential future events.
- ERM describes the role and responsibilities of risk officers and expands on the role of a company's board of directors.

Code of Practice for Information Security Management (ISO/IEC 17799/BS7799)

ISO 17799 is a code of practice for information security management. This code of practice takes a baseline approach to information security. It provides 127 information security guidelines structured under 10 major headings to enable readers to identify the security controls that are appropriate to their particular business or specific area of responsibility. The standard provides guidance on the following subjects:

- Security policy
- Security organisation
- Asset classification and control
- Personnel security

- Physical and environmental security
- Communications and operations management
- Access control
- System development and maintenance
- Business Continuity management
- Compliance.

BS7799-2 is a companion standard to ISO/IEC 17799. It is a management standard, based on risk assessment and the Plan-Do-Check-Act model, which are two vital ingredients of Corporate Governance. It provides a basis on which to build the management controls necessary to achieve an organisation's mission, to manage risk, to assure effective control and to seek improvements where appropriate.

ITIL

ITIL is the acronym for the 'IT Infrastructure Library' guidelines developed by the CCTA (now OGC) in Norwich, England, for the British government. ITIL is a best practice framework for IT Service Management and is seen as the *de facto* global standard in this area. For example, ITIL provides the foundation for the Microsoft Operations Framework (MOF) and for the HP IT Service Management Reference Model.

ITIL consists of a series of books giving best practice guidance for service management, with the guidelines describing what rather than how. Service management is tailored to the size, the internal culture and the requirements of the company. An important focus is the provision of quality IT services.

Best known ITIL books (figure 1.3) are the **Service Support** book, which describes the Service Desk and the Incident Management, Problem Management, Configuration Management, Change

Management and Release Management processes, and the
Service Delivery book, which describes processes for Capacity
Management, Financial Management for IT Services, Availability
Management, Service Level Management and IT Service Continuity
Management.

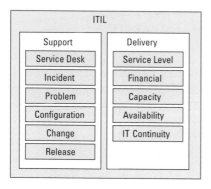

**Figure 1.3 Best known ITIL Processes (Note: the Service Desk is not a
process but an organisational unit)**

The other core ITIL books are shown in figure 1.4.

The book **Planning to Implement Service Management** explains
the steps necessary to identify how an organisation might expect to
benefit from ITIL and how to achieve these benefits.

The **ICT Infrastructure Management** book is concerned with the
processes, organisation and tools needed to provide a stable IT
and communications infrastructure.

The **Application Management book** is a guide for business users,
developers and service managers, and describes how applications

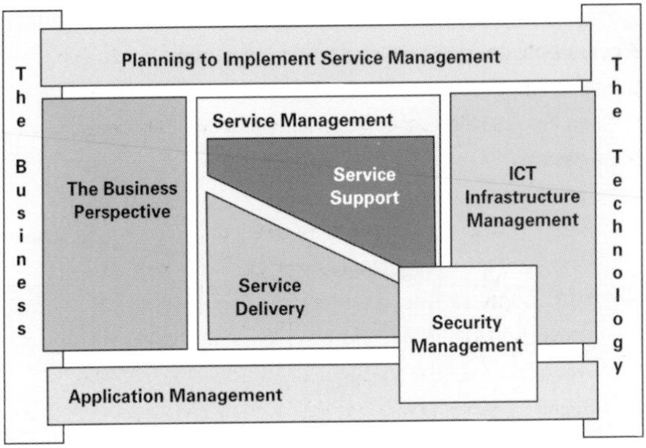

Figure 1.4 The ITIL publication structure (source OGC)

can be managed from a service management perspective.

Security Management is described in a separate book, and has connections with several of the other domains.

The **Business Perspective** book is to be published in 2004, and is concerned with helping business managers to understand IT service provision.

CMM / SPICE (ISO/IEC 15504)

The first Capability Maturity Model was developed by the Software Engineering Institute (SEI) of the Carnegie Mellon University and describes the principles and practices underlying software development process maturity. It was intended to help software organisations improve their software processes by following an evolutionary path from ad hoc, chaotic processes to mature, disciplined software processes. This CMM was organised into five maturity levels:

1. *Initial* - The software process is characterised as ad hoc, and

occasionally even chaotic. Few processes are defined, and success depends on individual effort and heroics.

2. *Repeatable* - Basic project management processes are established to track cost, schedule, and functionality. The necessary process discipline is in place to repeat earlier successes on projects with similar applications.

3. *Defined* - The software process for both management and engineering activities is documented, standardised, and integrated into a standard software process for the organisation. All projects use an approved, tailored version of the organisation's standard software process for developing and maintaining software.

4. *Managed* - Detailed measurements of the software process and product quality are collected. Both the software process and products are quantitatively understood and controlled.

5. *Optimising* - Continuous process improvement is enabled by quantitative feedback from the process and from piloting innovative ideas and technologies.

Predictability, effectiveness, and control of an organisation's software processes are believed to improve as the organisation moves up these five levels. While not rigorous, the empirical evidence to date supports this belief.

The idea of describing process maturity has expanded enormously since the first Software CMM was developed. Nowadays CMMs can be found for People, Software Acquisition, Systems Engineering, Integrated Product Development and IT Services. Several CMMs have been integrated by SEI into the Capability Maturity Model® Integration (CMMI℠). CMMI is consistent and compatible with ISO/IEC 15504, which is a framework for assessment methods. This standard results from the work of the Software Process Improvement and Capability determination (SPICE) initiative, which delivered a first draft in 1995.

CobiT uses a maturity model as a means of assessing the maturity of the processes described in the different CobiT domains and to help organisations set their maturity goals for these processes. The CobiT Maturity model knows the following levels:

0. *Non-existent* - There is a complete lack of any recognisable processes. The organisation has not even recognised that there is an issue to be addressed.

1. *Initial / Ad Hoc* - There is evidence that the organisation has recognised that the issues exist and need to be addressed. There are, however, no standardised processes, but instead there are ad hoc approaches applied on an individual or case-by-case basis. The overall approach to management is disorganised.

2. *Repeatable but Intuitive* - Processes have developed to the stage where similar procedures are followed by different individuals undertaking the same task. There is no formal training and the communication of standard procedures and responsibilities is left to the individual. There is a high degree of reliance on the knowledge of individuals and therefore errors are likely.

3. *Defined Process* - Procedures have been standardised and documented and communicated through training. It is however left to the individual to follow these processes and it is unlikely that deviations will be detected. The procedures themselves are not sophisticated but are a formalisation of existing practices.

4. *Managed and Measurable* - It is possible to monitor and measure compliance with procedures and to take action where processes appear not to be working effectively or efficiently. Processes are under improvement and provide good internal practice. Continuous improvement is beginning to be addressed. Automation and tools are used in a limited and fragmented way.

5. *Optimised* - Processes have been refined to a level of external best practice, based on results of continuous improvement and maturity modelling with other organisations. IT is used in an integrated way to automate the workflow, providing tools to improve

quality and effectiveness and making the organisation adaptive to its ever-changing environment.

Common Criteria (ISO/IEC 15408)

The Common Criteria represents the outcome of a series of efforts to develop criteria for evaluation of IT security that are broadly useful within the international community. In the 1980's and 1990's different countries worked upon developing their own criteria for security.

In June 1993, seven European and North American governmental organisations, constituting the Common Criteria project sponsoring organisations, pooled their efforts and began a joint activity to align their separate criteria into a single set of IT security criteria that could be widely used. This activity was named the Common Criteria Project. Its purpose was to resolve the conceptual and technical differences found in the source criteria and to deliver the results to ISO as a contribution to the international standard under development.

In 1999 ISO published its 'Evaluation Criteria for Information Technology Security' (ISO/IEC 15408). ISO continues the use of the term 'Common Criteria' within this document.

The Common Criteria is a means to define, assess, and measure the security aspects of ICT products. The Common Criteria supports understanding of 'what the product does' (security functionality) and 'how sure you are of that' (security assurance).

The Common Criteria are useful for product developers by providing them with the knowledge they need to design ICT products in such a way that they can pass an evaluation. For ICT products certified against Common Criteria, customers can be sure of which security aspects of the product were tested and how these aspects were tested.

EAL1	functionally tested
EAL2	structurally tested
EAL3	methodically tested and checked
EAL4	methodically designed, tested, and reviewed
EAL5	semiformally designed and tested
EAL6	semiformally verified design and tested
EAL7	formally verified design and tested

Table 1.2 Common Criteria evaluation assurance levels

The common criteria are used to certify so called Targets of Evaluation (TOE) against criteria resulting in an evaluation assurance level for the TOE (table 1.2).

Quality models (Deming, EFQM, BNQP, ISO9000)

Quality is addressed in a number of different models. Quality models aim at controlling and improving products and processes. While quality theory originates from business process environments, in many cases the ideas have also been adopted within IT.

Deming's work is very well known. He focused on process improvement in an industrial production environment as a means of improving product quality.

Deming created a diagram (figure 1.5) to illustrate this continuous process, known as the PDCA cycle for Plan, Do, Check, Act:

PLAN - Design or revise business process components to improve results.

DO - Implement the plan and measure its performance.

Figure 1.5 Deming Cycle

CHECK - Assess the measurements and report the results to decision makers.

ACT - Decide on changes needed to improve the process

Deming did his work on quality in the 1950's. Since that time several quality models have been developed. Some well known models will be compared here.

The **Baldridge National Quality Program (BNQP)** was started in 1987 to improve product and process quality within American organisations. Also in 1987 the **International Organization for Standardization (ISO)** issued a quality standard (ISO 9000) which was built on the specification of BS 5750. This standard has evolved into a family of ISO standards with regard to quality. The **EFQM Excellence Model** was introduced at the beginning of 1992 as the framework for assessing applications for the European Quality Award. It is the most widely used organisational framework in Europe and has become the basis for the majority of national and regional Quality Awards.

Each model has its own characteristics, but as shown in table 1.3, they also have many common principles.

Basic Principles of the 'Malcolm Baldridge' Model	EFQM fundamental concepts of excellence	ISO 9000: 2000 Quality Management Principles
Client-focused quality	Customer focus	Focus on your customers
Focusing on results	Results orientation	
Commitment from top management	Leadership & constancy of purpose	Provide leadership
Long-term vision of the future		
Valuation of people	People development & involvement	Involve your people
Social responsibility	Corporate social responsibility	
Management based on actions and processes	Management by processes & facts	Use a process approach
Proactive actions and rapid responses		
Continuous learning	Continuous learning, innovation & improvement	Encourage continual improvement
	Partnership development	Work with your suppliers
		Take a systems approach
		Get the facts before you decide

Table 1.3 Principles of quality models

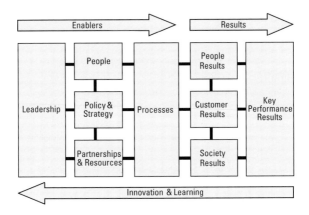

Figure 1.6 EFQM model (source EFQM)

As shown in the EFQM model (figure 1.6), quality is influenced by many factors.

Balanced Scorecard

The balanced scorecard is a *management system* that enables organisations to clarify their vision and strategy and translate them into action. It provides feedback about both the internal business processes and external outcomes enabling the continuous improvement of strategic performance and results. Kaplan and Norton describe the importance of the balanced scorecard as follows:

"The balanced scorecard retains traditional financial measures. But financial measures tell the story of past events, an adequate story for industrial age companies for which investments in long-term capabilities and customer relationships were not critical for success. These financial measures are inadequate, however, for guiding and evaluating the journey that information age companies must make to create future

value through investment in customers, suppliers,
employees, processes, technology, and innovation."

In their book *The Balanced Scorecard*, Kaplan and Norton set forth
a hypothesis about the chain of cause and effect that leads to
strategic success. There are four parts to this chain:

1. The foundation for strategic success has to do with people.
2. In a learning and growing organisation the people who are involved with the business processes on a daily basis can provide
   ideas for improving the processes.
3. Improved business processes lead to improved products and
   services. The balanced scorecard measures customer satisfaction, which is produced by improving processes.

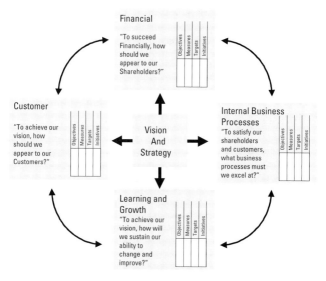

Figure 1.7 Business Balanced Scorecard (source BalancedScorecard.org)

4. Improved customer satisfaction leads to loyal customers and increased market share.

Based on this chain of cause and effect, the balanced scorecard offers an instrument for viewing the organisation from four perspectives. Metrics can be developed and data collected and analysed for each of these perspectives (see figure 1.7).

While the balanced scorecard has been developed as a business instrument, it is also used in IT.

The article 'The IT Balanced Scorecard and IT Governance', written by Van Grembergen, describes a cascade of balanced scorecards. He shows that a cascade of a Business Balanced Scorecard and IT Balanced Scorecards for the major IT processes can provide a measurement and management system that supports the IT Governance process: defining IT strategy, developing systems and operating systems (figure 1.8). The proposed cascade of balanced scorecards fuses business and IT and in this way supports the IT Governance process.

Figure 1.8 Balanced Scorecard (BSC) cascade (source: Van Grembergen)

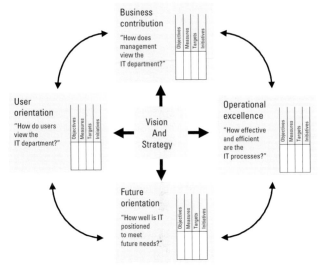

Figure 1.9 IT Balanced Scorecard

In his article Van Grembergen describes specific perspectives for IT, as depicted in the IT Balanced Scorecard (figure 1.9).

The *User orientation* perspective represents the user evaluation of IT. The *Operational excellence* perspective represents the IT processes employed to develop and deliver the applications. The *Future orientation* perspective represents the human and technology resources needed by IT to deliver its services. The *Business contribution* perspective captures the business value of the IT investments.

CobiT

CobiT stands for Control Objectives for Information and related Technology. CobiT is a model for control of the full IT. The name of the product already betrays its auditing background. This model was originally developed by the Information Systems Audit and Control Foundation (ISACF®), the research institute for the Information Systems Audit and Control Association (ISACA®). In 2003 Information System Audit and Control Foundation (ISACF) changed its name to the IT Governance Institute (ITGI®). Therefore, all marks formally held by the Foundation are now held by the IT Governance Institute.

CobiT development started in 1994, with a first version published in 1996, and subsequent versions in 1998 and 2000.

Originally, CobiT targeted auditors, end-users and management.

COBIT is a model for control of the IT environment. In developing COBIT, standards from different sources have been used, that each cover a part of the information systems control field.

COBIT supports IT Governance by providing a comprehensive description of the control objectives for IT processes and by offering the possibility of examining the maturity of these processes.

It helps in understanding, assessing and managing the risks together with the benefits associated with information and related IT. COBIT provides an IT Governance instrument that allows managers to bridge the gap with respect to control requirements, Information Systems (IS) & Information Technology (IT) issues and business risks, in order to communicate that level of control to stakeholders. It enables the development of clear policy and good practice for the control of IT throughout organisations.

COBIT Target Groups

According to ITGI, COBIT is primarily intended for management, business users of IT and auditors. Additionally, a wide range of other disciplines, roles and functions can benefit from the guidelines provided. For instance, business and IT consultants can provide management with advice on control issues and IT Service Management professionals can use knowledge about control objectives in order to improve their processes.

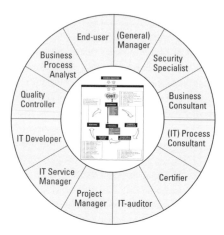

Figure 2.1 Possible target groups

The main target groups are described in the following paragraphs.

Managers

Within organisations managers are the ones that hold executive responsibility for operation of the enterprise. They need information in order to control the internal operations and to direct business processes. IT is an integral part of business operations. CobiT can help both business and IT managers to balance risk and control investment in an often unpredictable IT environment.

End-users

Most organisations realise that having the right IT services is the responsibility of the business process owner. This is even the case when the delivery of IT services is delegated to internal or external service providers. CobiT offers a framework to obtain assurance on the security and controls of IT services provided by internal or external parties.

Auditors

In order to provide independent assurance of the quality and applicability of controls, organisations employ auditors. Often an audit committee at the board or top management level directs auditing. CobiT helps auditors to structure and substantiate their opinions and provide advice to management on how to improve internal controls.

Business and IT Consultants

New frameworks and methods, e.g. on IT Governance often originate outside the enterprise. Business and IT consultants can bring this knowledge into the enterprise and thus provide advice to business and IT management on improving IT Governance.

IT Service Management professionals

In the IT Service Management community, ITIL is the dominant framework. CobiT helps to further improve IT Service Management by providing a framework that covers the complete lifecycle of IT systems and services.

CobiT Structure

The CobiT structure is represented by the CobiT cube, which depicts three interrelated viewpoints.

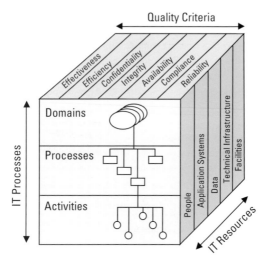

Figure 2.2 IT Governance Cube (Source: ITGI COBIT Cube)

Each viewpoint is described in one of the following paragraphs.

COBIT Domains and Processes

The COBIT processes have been ordered in four distinct domains, which together form a cycle. This cycle has incorrectly been compared to the Deming quality cycle, but shows a better match with the management cycle as described by Hopstaken & Kranendonk in 1988. In their original publication Hopstaken & Kranendonk presented the following four groups of processes:

- Strategy, Modelling & Planning
- Realisation
- Delivery & Support
- Monitoring & Correction

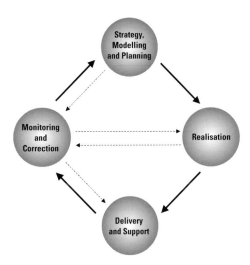

Figure 2.3 Management Cycle (Hopstaken & Kranendonk, 1988)

Strategy, Modelling & Planning provides Monitoring & Correction
with the standards by which Realisation and Delivery & Support can
be assessed. From Monitoring there is a double-loop feedback. In
the first loop Realisation and Delivery & Support are provided with
feedback in order to correct the process results. The second feed-
back-loop provides the Strategy, Modelling & Planning processes
with input needed for improvement of the next cycle.

The four CobiT domains can be projected almost seamlessly onto
this management cycle.

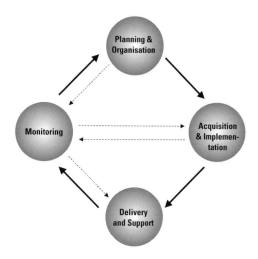

Figure 2.4 CobiT mapped onto Management Cycle

For each CobiT domain a number of processes have been identified. These are listed in the following table. Further information about the processes and activities can be found in chapter 4.

Each domain is characterised in a short description.

Planning and Organisation (PO)

This domain covers strategy and tactics and is concerned with the identification of the way IT can best contribute to the achievement of business objectives. The realisation of the strategic vision has to be planned, communicated and managed from different points of view (e.g. information architecture and technological direction) and a proper organisation and technological infrastructure must be in place.

Planning and Organisation (PO)

PO1	Define a Strategic IT Plan
PO2	Define the Information Architecture
PO3	Determine Technological Direction
PO4	Define the IT Organisation and Relationships
PO5	Manage the IT Investment
PO6	Communicate Management Aims and Direction
PO7	Manage Human Resources
PO8	Ensure Compliance with External Requirements
PO9	Assess and Manage Risks
PO10	Manage Projects
PO11	Manage Quality

Acquisition and Implementation (AI)

AI1	Identify Automated Solutions
AI2	Acquire and Maintain Application Software
AI3	Acquire and Maintain Technology Infrastructure
AI4	Develop and Maintain Procedures
AI5	Install and Accredit Systems
AI6	Manage Changes

Delivery and Support (DS)

DS1	Define and Manage Service Levels
DS2	Manage Third-Party Services
DS3	Manage Performance and Capacity
DS4	Ensure Continuous Service
DS5	Ensure Systems Security
DS6	Identify and Allocate Costs
DS7	Educate and Train Users
DS8	Assist and Advise Customers
DS9	Manage the Configuration
DS10	Manage Problems and Incidents
DS11	Manage Data
DS12	Manage Facilities
DS13	Manage Operations

Monitoring (M)

M1	Monitor the Processes
M2	Assess Internal Control Adequacy
M3	Obtain Independent Assurance
M4	Provide for Independent Audit

Table 2.1 Processes in the four management domains. (Source: ITGI CobiT Framework)

The processes PO1 (Define a Strategic IT Plan), PO2 (Define the Information Architecture), PO3 (Determine Technological direction) and PO4 (Define the IT organisation and Relationships) make up the strategic cluster that is at the heart of the Planning and Organisation domain (figure 2.5). These four processes have to be performed interactively and iteratively. Choices made in one process can influence the outcome of the other processes.

Business requirements are input to the strategic cluster, as well as the external requirements, which are first processed in PO8 (Ensure Compliance with External Requirements).

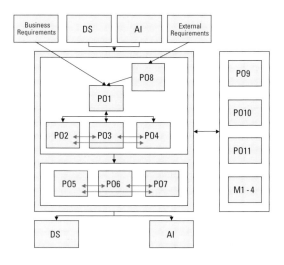

Figure 2.5 Structure Planning & Organisation domain

The results of the strategic cluster are input to PO5 (Manage the IT Investment), PO6 (Communicate Management Aims and Directions) and PO7 (Manage Human Resources).

The box on the right of this figure describes PO9 (Assess and Manage Risks), PO10 (Manage Projects), PO11 (Manage Quality) and the monitoring cluster. These processes have been set apart because they are a general resource to not only the processes in the Planning & Organisation cluster, but also to the processes in the other clusters.

Acquisition and Implementation (AI)

In order to realise the IT strategy, IT solutions need to be identified, developed or acquired, as well as implemented and integrated into the business process. In addition, to make sure that the life cycle is

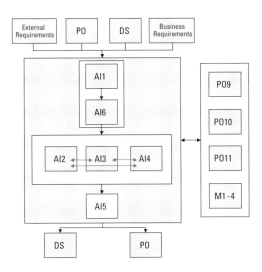

Figure 2.6 Structure Acquisition & Implementation domain

continued for existing systems, this domain covers changes in and maintenance of these systems.

Based upon the information architecture and technological direction defined in the Planning & Organisation cluster and upon the requirements from business and external sources, process AI1 (Identify Automated Solutions) defines the changes needed in the IT infrastructure. AI6 (Manage Changes) ensures that these changes are dealt with in a responsible, non-disruptive manner. The development cluster processes AI2 (Acquire and Maintain Application Software), AI3 (Acquire and Maintain Technology Infrastructure) and AI4 (Develop and Maintain Procedures) ensure that as a result of these processes a working information system is delivered. The process AI5 (Install and Accredit Systems) takes care of implementing an accredited system into the operational environment.

A separate box describes PO9 (Assess and Manage Risks), PO10 (Manage Projects), PO11 (Manage Quality) and the monitoring cluster as a general resource to the processes in this domain.

Delivery and Support (DS)

This domain is concerned with the delivery of required services, which range from traditional operations over security and continuity aspects to training. In order to deliver services, the necessary support processes must be set up. This domain includes the processing of data by application systems, which is often classified under application controls.

The process DS1 (Define and Manage Service Levels) is a key-process in this cluster, because it links IT Delivery & Support to the business by way of defined and agreed upon Service Level Agreements (figure 2.7). The agreements directly influence DS2 (Manage Third-Party Services). Both DS1 and DS2 are directly related to DS6

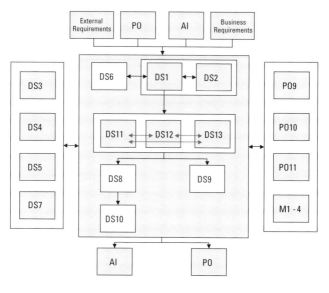

Figure 2.7 Structure Delivery & Support domain

(Identify and Allocate Costs), because of the financial implications of both service level agreements and external agreements.

DS1 provides the operation cluster processes DS11 (Manage Data), DS12 (Manage Facilities) and DS13 (Manage Operations) with performance criteria against which the quantity and quality of service provided will be measured.

DS8 (Assist an Advise Customers) provides a primary contact point for users with regard to any problem experienced with the operational system. DS10 (Manage Problems and Incidents) takes care that incidents and problems are resolved in a professional way, while DS9 (Manage the Configuration) takes care that the operational IT environment is correctly documented.

Processes DS3 (Manage Performance and Capacity), DS4 (Ensure Continuous Service), DS5 (Ensure Systems Security) and DS7 (Educate and Train Users) support the other processes in this domain.

A separate box describes PO9 (Assess and Manage Risks), PO10 (Manage Projects), PO11 (Manage Quality) and the monitoring cluster as a general resource to the processes in this domain.

Monitoring (M)

All IT processes need to be regularly assessed over time for their quality and compliance with control requirements. This domain addresses management oversight of the organisation's control process and independent assurance provided by internal and external audit or obtained from alternative sources.

M1 (Monitor the Processes) is the primary monitoring process and measures all processes against performance indicators (figure 2.8). It also ensures that corrective action is taken. M2 (Assess Internal Control Adequacy) monitors for internal control objectives. While M1 and M2 are performed within the organisation, M3 (Obtain Independent Assurance) ensures that external assurance is provided for.

M4 (Provide for Independent Audit) might as well have been part of the Planning & Organisation domain, because it provides for the planning & organisation of monitoring.

A separate box describes PO9 (Assess and Manage Risks), PO10 (Manage Projects) and PO11 (Manage Quality) as a general resource to the processes in this domain.

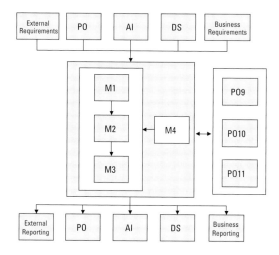

Figure 2.8 Structure Monitoring domain

IT resources

In general literature five classes of IT resources are identified:

- *People* - the human resources needed to plan, organise, acquire, deliver, support and monitor information systems and services.
- *Application systems* - including both manual and programmed procedures.
- *Data* - the representation of relevant external and internal objects. Structured and non-structured, graphics, sound, etc.
- *Technical infrastructure* - covering hardware, operating systems, database management systems, networking software, etc.
- *Facilities* - the resources to house and support business and information systems.

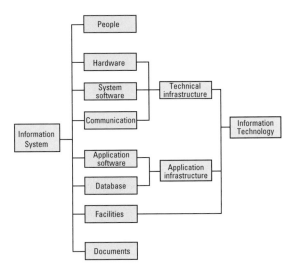

Figure 2.9 The IS decomposition tree according to the Compendium IT Service Management

Each process within CobiT deals with the control of one or more IT resources. Figure 2.9 shows how the information system can be decomposed into meaningful components.

Quality Criteria

An underpinning concept for CobiT is that control of IT is approached by looking at the information that is needed to support the business requirements. In establishing the criteria for information, CobiT analysed existing and known reference models:

- *Quality Requirements*:
  - Quality
  - Cost
  - Delivery

- *Fiduciary Requirements (COSO report)*:
  - Effectiveness and Efficiency of operations
  - Reliability of Information
  - Compliance with laws and regulations
- *Security Requirements*:
  - Confidentiality
  - Integrity
  - Availability

Quality has been retained primarily for its negative aspect (no faults, reliability, etc.) and this is also captured to a large extent by the Integrity criterion. The positive but less tangible aspects of quality (style, attractiveness, look and feel, performing beyond expectations, etc.) are largely covered by other criteria. The usability aspect of quality is covered by the Effectiveness criterion. The delivery aspect of quality was considered to overlap with the Availability aspect of the security requirements and also to some extent with Effectiveness and Efficiency. Finally, cost is also considered covered by Efficiency.

For the Fiduciary Requirements, ITGI used COSO's well-accepted definitions for effectiveness and efficiency of operations, reliability of information and compliance with laws and regulations, rather then attempting new definitions. However, Reliability of Information was expanded to include all information - not just financial information.

With respect to the Security Requirements, CobiT identified Confidentiality, Integrity and Availability as the key elements - these same three elements, it was found, are used worldwide in describing IT security requirements.

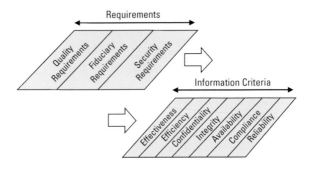

**Figure 2.10 Transition from requirements to quality criteria
(Source: ITGI CobiT Framework)**

For information, a number of quality criteria are identified. CobiT also refers to these as Information Criteria.

Fot this pocket guide, the quality criteria are defined as follows:
- *Effectiveness* - the extent to which the information serves the defined objectives.
- *Efficiency* - the extent to which activities with regard to the pro-vision of information are carried out at an acceptable cost and effort.
- *Confidentiality* - the extent to which data is only accessible to a well-defined group of authorised persons.
- *Integrity* - the extent to which data corresponds with the actual situation represented by that data.
- *Availability* - the extent to which a system or service is available to the intended users at the required times.
- *Compliance* - the extent to which processes act in accordance with those laws, regulations and contractual arrangements to which the process is subject.
- *Reliability of Information* - relates to the provision of appropriate

information for management to operate the entity and for management to exercise its financial and compliance reporting responsibilities.

The business process owners define what information is needed in order to meet their business objectives. CobiT, as an instrument for governing the IT environment, identifies the processes within the four domains required to meet the quality criteria relevant to the business, using the necessary IT resources.

The overall CobiT structure is depicted in figure 2.11, which also shows its relationship with Business Objectives.

BUSINESS OBJECTIVES

IT GOVERNANCE

CobiT

INFORMATION

- effectiveness
- efficiency
- confidentiality
- integrity
- availability
- compliance
- reliability

PO1 Define a Strategic IT Plan
PO2 Define the Information Architecture
PO3 Determine Technological Direction
PO4 Define the IT Organisation and Relationships
PO5 Manage the IT Investment
PO6 Communicate Management Aims and Direction
PO7 Manage Human Resources
PO8 Ensure Compliance with External Requirements
PO9 Assess and Manage Risks
PO10 Manage Projects
PO11 Manage Quality

M1 Monitor the Processes
M2 Assess Internal Control Adequacy
M3 Obtain Independent Assurance
M4 Provide for Independent Audit

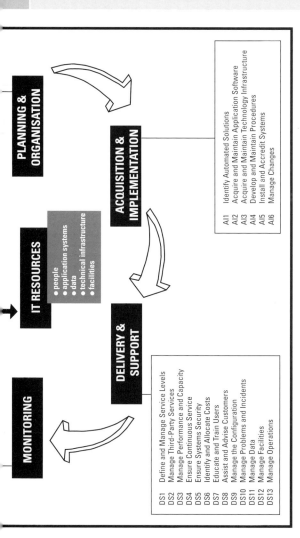

PLANNING & ORGANISATION

ACQUISITION & IMPLEMENTATION

AI1 Identify Automated Solutions
AI2 Acquire and Maintain Application Software
AI3 Acquire and Maintain Technology Infrastructure
AI4 Develop and Maintain Procedures
AI5 Install and Accredit Systems
AI6 Manage Changes

IT RESOURCES
- people
- application systems
- data
- technical infrastructure
- facilities

DELIVERY & SUPPORT

DS1 Define and Manage Service Levels
DS2 Manage Third-Party Services
DS3 Manage Performance and Capacity
DS4 Ensure Continuous Service
DS5 Ensure Systems Security
DS6 Identify and Allocate Costs
DS7 Educate and Train Users
DS8 Assist and Advise Customers
DS9 Manage the Configuration
DS10 Manage Problems and Incidents
DS11 Manage Data
DS12 Manage Facilities
DS13 Manage Operations

MONITORING

Figure 2.11 CobiT IT Processes defined within the four domains (Source: ITGI CobiT Framework)

3 COBIT Publications

The current CobiT (version 3) consists of the following books:

- Executive Summary
- Framework
- Management Guidelines
- Control Objectives
- Audit Guidelines
- Implementation Tool Set

The coherence between these books is shown in figure 3.1.

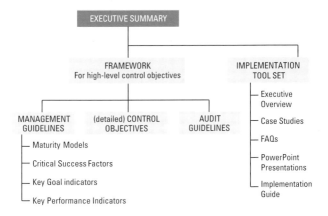

Figure 3.1 COBIT Family of Products (Source: ITGI COBIT Framework)

Each book is aimed at a specific audience, which is described in table 3.1.

Book Title	Audience
Executive Summary	Senior executives (CEO, CFO, COO, CIO)
Framework	Senior operational management (directors of IT/IS audit/controls)
Management Guidelines	Senior operational management, Director of IS, mid-level IT management and IT audit/control managers
Control Objectives	Middle management (mid-level IT Management and IS audit/controls managers/seniors)
Audit Guidelines	Line management and controls practitioner (applications or operations manager and auditor)
Implementation Tool Set	Director of IS and audit/control, Mid-level IS management and IS audit/control managers

Table 3.1 Audience for CobiT books (Source ISACA presentation)

Since 2000, in addition to the CobiT revision, a number of CobiT related products have been published:

- Board briefing on IT Governance (2001)
- Information Security Governance: Guidance for Boards of Directors and Executive Management (2001)
- IT Governance Executive Summary (2002)
- IT Strategy Committee (2002)
- CobiT Online (2003)
- CobiT Quickstart (2003)
- IT Governance Implementation Guide using CobiT (2003)
- IT Control Practice Statements (2004)

CoʙiT is a living standard. At this moment there are several projects working on different aspects of CoʙiT. Information on new developments can always be found on the ITGI website.

Most publications can be downloaded from the ISACA (www.isaca.org) and IT Governance Institute (www.itgi.org) Web sites. Download of the Audit Guidelines is restricted to ISACA members.

The next paragraphs briefly describe the CoʙiT documents.

Executive Summary

The Executive Summary is a thin booklet that provides basic information about CoʙiT.

It provides a brief overview of the CoʙiT framework and its purpose and describes the place of IT Governance within an Enterprise Governance context. It also introduces some basic definitions that are important to the understanding of CoʙiT. In particular:

- *Control* is defined as the policies, procedures, practices and organisational structures designed to provide reasonable assurance that business objectives will be achieved and that undesired events will be prevented or detected and corrected.
- An *IT Control Objective* is defined as a statement of the desired result or purpose to be achieved by implementing control procedures in a particular IT activity.
- *IT Governance* is defined as a structure of relationships and processes to direct and control the enterprise in order to achieve the enterprise's goals by adding value while balancing risk versus return over IT and its processes.

Framework and Control Objectives

Because the publications 'CobiT Framework' and 'CobiT Control Objectives' are closely related, they are discussed in combination. In fact this last book adds an extra level of detail to the high-level control objectives from the framework.

The CobiT Framework is written for senior operational management. The CobiT Control Objectives are aimed at middle management.

The framework starts with the following premise:

> *In order to provide the information that the organisation needs to achieve its objectives, IT resources need to be managed by a set of naturally grouped processes.*

The framework describes high-level control objectives for each process within the CobiT domains. By addressing these objectives, the business process owner can ensure that the IT environment is adequately controlled.

Figure 3.2 shows, by IT process and domain, which information criteria are impacted by the high-level control objectives. It further indicates which IT resources are applicable. The Information criteria and IT resources have already been explained in Chapter 1.

When looking at control measures for processes and applicable information criteria, not all information criteria will satisfy the different business requirements for information to the same degree:
- *Primary (P)* - the defined control objective directly impacts the information criterion concerned.
- *Secondary (S)* - the defined control objective satisfies only to a lesser extent the information criterion concerned.

Information Criteria — P = primary, S = secondary. IT Resources marked with ✓.

DOMAIN		PROCESS	effectiveness	efficiency	confidentiality	integrity	availability	compliance	reliability	people	appl. systems	technical infra.	facilities	data
Planning & Organisation	PO1	Define a Strategic IT Plan	P	S						✓	✓	✓	✓	✓
	PO2	Define the Information Architecture	P	S	S						✓			✓
	PO3	Determine Technological Direction	P	S		S						✓	✓	
	PO4	Define the IT Organisation and Relationships	P	S						✓				
	PO5	Manage the IT Investment	P	P						✓	✓	✓	✓	
	PO6	Communicate Management Aims and Direction	P					S	S	✓				
	PO7	Manage Human Resources	P	P						✓				
	PO8	Ensure Compliance with External Requirements	P	S	P	P	P	P	S	✓				
	PO9	Assess and Manage Risks	P	P	S	P	P	S	S	✓	✓	✓	✓	✓
	PO10	Manage Projects	P	P						✓	✓	✓	✓	✓
	PO11	Manage Quality	P	P		P			S	✓		✓	✓	
Aquisition & Implementation	AI1	Identify Automated Solutions	P	S							✓		✓	
	AI2	Acquire and Maintain Application Software	P	P		S		S	S		✓	✓		
	AI3	Acquire and Maintain Technology Infrastructure	P	P		S						✓		

AI4	Develop and Maintain Procedures	P	P			S		S	✓		✓	✓	✓
AI5	Install and Accredit Systems	P				S			✓	✓	✓	✓	✓
AI6	Manage Changes	P			P	P		S	✓	✓	✓	✓	✓
Delivery &	**DS1** Define and Manage Service Levels	P	P	S	S	S	S	S	✓	✓		✓	✓
Support	**DS2** Manage Third-Party Services	P	P	S	S	S	S	S	✓	✓	✓	✓	✓
	DS3 Manage Performance and Capacity	P	P			S			✓		✓	✓	
	DS4 Ensure Continuous Service	P	S			P			✓	✓	✓	✓	✓
	DS5 Ensure Systems Security			P	P	S		S	✓	✓	✓		✓
	DS6 Identify and Allocate Costs		P			P		P	✓	✓	✓		✓
	DS7 Educate and Train Users	P	S						✓				
	DS8 Assist and Advise Customers	P	P						✓				
	DS9 Manage the Configuration	P			S	S		S		✓	✓		✓
	DS10 Manage Problems and Incidents	P	P		S	S			✓	✓	✓		✓
	DS11 Manage Data			P	P			P					✓
	DS12 Manage Facilities			P	P							✓	
	DS13 Manage Operations	P	P	S	S				✓		✓	✓	✓
Monitoring	**M1** Monitor the Processes	P	P	S	S	S	S	S	✓	✓	✓	✓	✓
	M2 Assess Internal Control Adequacy	P	P	S	S	P	S	S	✓	✓	✓	✓	✓
	M3 Obtain Independent Assurance	P	P	S	S	P	S	S	✓	✓	✓	✓	✓
	M4 Provide for Independent Audit	P	P	S	S	P	S	S	✓	✓	✓	✓	✓

Figure 3.2 Control Objectives Summary Table (Source: ITGI CobiT Framework)

- *Blank* - when not indicated as primary or secondary, requirements for the information criterion could be applicable; however, requirements are more appropriately satisfied by another criterion in this process and/or by another process.

Not all control measures will necessarily impact the different IT resources to the same degree. Therefore, CobiT indicates the applicability of the IT resources that are specifically managed by the process under consideration (not those that merely take part in the process). Organisations should carefully examine these control objectives to see which ones are most applicable in their own, specific situation.

The CobiT Control Objectives book looks at the control objectives for each process in more detail. Over 300 detailed control objectives are described in order to provide control measures for each process.

The number of detailed control objectives for each process varies. For some processes only three or four detailed control objectives have been defined. For other processes up to 30 detailed control objectives can be found.

Management Guidelines

The Management Guidelines book provides directives for management in directing and managing IT activities. The objective is to reach a balance between managing risk and realising business benefits. To accomplish this, management needs to identify the most important activities to be performed, set performance goals, measure progress towards achieving goals and determine how well the IT activities are performing.

The Management Guidelines have been written to enable enterprise

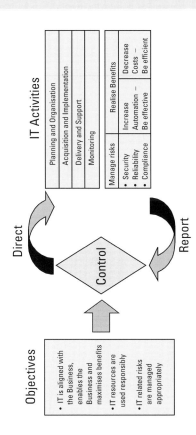

Figure 3.3 IT Governance (Source: ITGI CobiT Framework)

and IT management to deal more effectively with the needs and
requirements of IT Governance. The guidelines are action-oriented
and generic and they provide management with direction for:

- getting the enterprise's information and related processes under
  control;
- monitoring achievement of organisational goals;

- monitoring performance within each IT process;
- benchmarking organisational achievement.

Every Management Guideline provides a number of elements for each of the 34 CobiT processes:

- *Process* identification.
- *Goal* statement for the process.
- *IT Resources* - with an indication of relevance to this process.
- *Information Criteria* - with an indication of relative importance.
- *Critical Success Factors (CSF)* - factors that define the most important management-oriented results required to achieve control over the IT processes.
- *Key Goal Indicators (KGI)* - indicators that define measures with regard to information quality criteria that tell management (ex-post) whether an IT process has achieved its business requirements.
- *Key Performance Indicators (KPI)* - lead indicators that define measures of how well the IT process is performing with regard to the goal to be reached.
- *Maturity model* - as an instrument to analyse the current position, the position relative to 'best in class', and the position regarding international standards. The maturity model can be used to set targets for future development, based upon where the organisation wants to be on the scale.

Audit Guidelines

The audit guidelines enable the review of IT processes against the recommended detailed control objectives to provide management assurance and/or advice for improvement. They provide guidance for preparing audit plans that are integrated with the CobiT Framework and Control Objectives.

Using the Audit Guidelines helps the auditor to underpin his conclusions, because CobiT is based on authoritative criteria from standards and best practice statements from private and public standard setting bodies.

While explaining what the Audit Guidelines are, it is prudent to indicate their limitations:

1. The Audit Guidelines are not intended as a tool for creating an overall audit plan. Such a plan considers factors like including past weaknesses, risks to the organisation, known incidents, new developments and strategic choices.
2. The Audit Guidelines are not intended as a tool to teach auditing, even though they incorporate the generally accepted basics of general and IT auditing.
3. The Audit Guidelines do not attempt to explain in detail how computerised planning, assessment, analysis and documentation tools can be used to support and automate the audit of IT processes.
4. The Audit Guidelines are neither exhaustive nor definitive, but will evolve together with CobiT.

The general structure for auditing IT processes (figure 3.4) is:
- *Obtain an understanding of risks* related to business requirements and relevant control measures.
- *Evaluate the appropriateness* of stated controls.
- *Assess compliance* by testing whether the stated controls are working as prescribed, consistently and continuously.
- *Substantiate the risk* of control objectives not being met by using analytical techniques and/or consulting alternative sources.

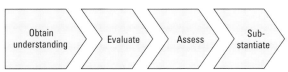

Figure 3.4 Audit Activities

This structure appears within the CobiT generic audit guidelines as a first level of detail. The second level, which contains detailed audit guidelines for each IT process, is described according to the same structure.

At a third level, the audit guidelines may be complemented with audit attention points pertaining to local conditions. These can be derived from:

- Sector specific criteria
- Industry standards
- Platform specific elements
- Detailed control techniques employed.

After defining what is going to be audited and where assurance is to be provided, the most appropriate approach or strategy for carrying out the audit work has to be developed:

- Determine the scope of the audit.
- Identify the information requirements of particular relevance to the business processes.
- Identify the inherent IT risks and overall level of control, which can be associated with the business process.
- On the basis of the information obtained, select the relevant CobiT processes and resources that apply to them.
- Determine an audit strategy and further elaborate on this basis, e.g., is one going for a controls based approach or for a substantive approach.
- Finally, consider all the steps, tasks and decision points to perform the audit.

Implementation Tool Set

The Implementation Tool Set contains lessons-learned from those organisations that have quickly and successfully applied CobiT in their work environments. It is intended for the director of IT and audit/control, mid-level IT management and IT audit/control managers.

The Implementation Toolset describes a way of implementing CoBIT in organisations and discusses:
- Stakeholders
- Why an organisation should adopt CoBIT
- CoBIT's scope and limitations.

The Implementation Tool Set covers the title IT Governance Implementation Guide using CoBIT. This guide provides readers with a methodology, using CoBIT, for implementing and improving IT governance.

In addition to the IT Governance Implementation Guide using CoBIT, the Tool Set contains tools to assist in analysing an organisation's IT control environment. The tools that are described are:
- IT Governance Self-Assessment
- Management IT-IS concerned with Diagnostic
- IT Control Diagnostic.

IT Governance Implementation Guide using CoBIT

The objective of this guide is to provide readers with a methodology for implementing or improving IT governance, using CoBIT. It will support the reader's role whether it relates to management, compliance, risk, performance, security or assurance of IT.

The guide is focused on a generic methodology for implementing IT governance, covering the following subjects:
- Why IT governance is important and why organisations should implement it
- The IT governance life cycle

- The CobiT framework
- How CobiT is linked to IT governance and how cobiT enables the implementation of IT governance
- The stakeholders who have an interest in IT governance
- A road map for implementing IT governance using CobiT

The guide is supported by an implementation tool kit, containing a variety of resources, including planning, documenting and reporting templates-all the templates needed to support the activities identified in the implementation road map. It also includes self-assessment, measurement, diagnostic and decision support tools; case studies and presentations.

CobiT Quickstart™

CobiT, in its complete form, can be a bit overwhelming for those who operate with a small IT staff and who may not have the resources to implement all of CobiT. This version of CobiT is a subset of the entire CobiT volume. Only those control objectives that are considered the most critical are included, so that implementation of CobiT's fundamental principles can take place easily, effectively and relatively quickly.

This special version of CobiT is a baseline for many small or medium enterprises (SMEs) and other organisations where IT is not mission-critical or essential for survival. It can also serve as a starting point for other enterprises in their move towards an appropriate level of control and governance of IT.

CobiT Online®

CobiT Online is, as its name implies, an online version of CobiT. This product allows users to customise a version of CobiT just right for their own enterprise, then store and manipulate that version as desired.

IT Control Practice Statements

The IT control practice statements are being developed as a supplement to the CobiT publications. They are meant to expand the capabilities of CobiT by providing the practitioner with an additional level of detail. The current IT processes, business information requirements and detailed control objectives define *what* needs to be done to implement an effective control structure. The IT control practices provide the more detailed *how* and *why*, needed by management, service providers, end users and control professionals to implement highly specific controls based on an analysis of operational and IT risks. The CobiT conceptual framework is thus extended with a more specific implementation focus.

Other publications

Board Briefing on IT Governance

This Board Briefing on IT Governance is addressed to boards of directors, supervisory boards, audit committees, chief executive officers, chief information officers and other executive management.

The board briefing was developed because the complexity of IT and the intangible value of information make IT a more difficult area to govern. It will help non-specialist directors and managers understand why IT Governance is important, what the issues are and what management's responsibility is for managing them.

It includes:

- A summarised background on governance
- Where IT Governance fits in the larger context of Enterprise Governance
- A simple framework with which to think about IT Governance and the different domains it covers:
  - Strategic alignment of IT with the business
  - Value delivery of IT
  - Management of IT risks
  - IT resource management
  - Performance measurement of IT
- Questions that should be asked
- Good practices and Critical Success Factors
- Performance measures board members can track
- A maturity model against which to benchmark the enterprise

IT Governance Executive Summary

The IT Governance Executive Summary gives a short introduction on IT Governance and its relevance within Enterprise Governance. It contains references to the *Board Briefing on IT Governance* and to *Information Security Governance: Guidance for Boards of Directors and Executive Management*.

IT Strategy Committee

This six page information brochure discusses reasons for deploying an IT Strategy committee as an instrument to assist the board in governing and overseeing the enterprise's IT-related matters. It covers the Committee's goal, responsibility and authority and distinguishes between an IT Strategy Committee and an IT Steering Committee.

Information Security Governance

The growth and success of nearly all enterprises rely on harnessing IT for secure, profitable use. All enterprises benefit from an integrated and comprehensive approach to risk management, security and control.

As organisations continue to take advantage of the opportunities available through global networking, and need to comply with existing or new security laws and regulations, difficult decisions arise about how much money to invest in IT security and control. Enterprises must consider the best ways to offer flexibility to customers and trading partners, yet ensure security of critical information and systems for all their users.

While executive management has the responsibility to consider and respond to these issues, boards of directors will increasingly be expected to make information security an intrinsic part of governance, preferably integrated with the processes they have in place to govern IT.

This guide is written to address these issues and covers fundamental questions like:

- What is information security?
- Why is it important?
- Who is responsible for it?

It also provides practical, pragmatic advice on:

- Questions to ask to uncover potential security weaknesses
- What information security governance should deliver
- How to implement information security
- How to measure your enterprise's maturity level relative to information security governance

4 COBIT Process descriptions

Introduction

A powerful and central theme in COBIT is the focus on IT processes.
But although processes in COBIT are important, knowledge about
these processes is scattered over many publications.

In this IT Governance Pocket Guide all processes were described
briefly. The publication 'IT Governance - An Introduction' describes
each process in more detail.

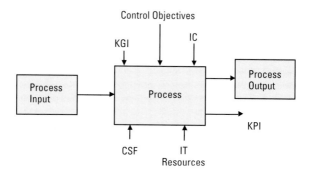

Figure 4.1 Generic Process Structure

The analysis of each process includes a set of formal characteristics:

1 *Introduction* - a short description of the process, supported by a
   diagram.
2 *Goal* - what the process intends to achieve.
3 *Key Goal Indicators* - the most important indicators that the
   process has achieved its goal.
4 *Detailed Control Objectives* - detailed Control Objectives that are
   the key to achieving process goals.
5 *Inputs* - the most important inputs to the process.
6 *Outputs* - the most important outputs from the process.

7   *Information Criteria* - the manner in which the information criteria
    impact the process (primary, secondary, blank).
8   *IT resources* - the IT resources that the process deals with.
9   *Activities* - the activities contained within the process (see figure
    4.2).
10 *Process Control* - An essential part of each process is monitor-
    ing the process steps. Because this is standard for each
    process, the monitoring will not be included in the detailed fig-
    ures within each process description.
    - *Functions and responsibilities* - the controlling functions and
      responsibilities that can be defined for the process.
    - *Key Performance Indicators* - the most useful performance in-
      dicators for this process.
    - *Reporting* - Suitable control reporting for the process.
11 *Relationships with other processes* - How the process described
    is related to other processes (see figure 4.3).
12 *Costs and Benefits*:
    - *Costs* - The major cost drivers for this process.
    - *Benefits* - The benefits to be gained from controlling this
      process.
13 *Critical Success Factors and Bottlenecks*:
    - *Critical Success Factors* - The most important Critical Suc-
      cess Factors for the process.
    - *Bottlenecks* - The most important possible problems for the
      process
14 *Maturity Model* - The criteria for the different levels of maturity for
    this process

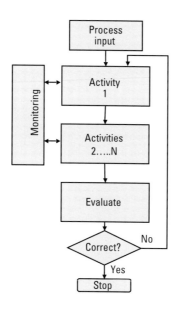

Figure 4.2 Generic Activity Model

This Pocket Guide includes only items 2) Goal, 6) Outputs, 9) Activities, and 11) Relationships with other processes. For each process a workflow diagram is provided. In this workflow diagram the activities are clustered into meaningful steps. A full set of descriptions will be found in 'IT Governance - an Introduction', the training book that follows this pocket guide in 2004.

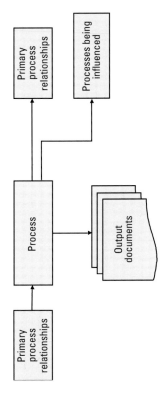

Figure 4.3 Generic Relationships Structure

Diagrams on the relationships with other processes have been developed as well. Both kinds of diagrams are additional to other sources that were used for this pocket guide.

PO   Planning and Organisation

PO1   Define a Strategic IT Plan

Goal

To strike an optimum balance of information technology opportunities and IT business requirements as well as ensuring its further accomplishment.

Activities

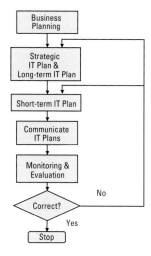

Figure 4.4   Activities of 'Define a Strategic IT Plan'

The following activities are carried out in the IT process 'Define a Strategic IT Plan':

- Create Strategic IT Plan
- Create Long-term IT Plan
- Create Short-term IT Plan

- Assessment of Existing Systems
- Communicate IT Plans
- Evaluate IT Plans
- Monitor process

Relationships with other processes

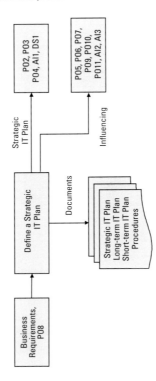

Figure 4.5 Relationships of 'Define a Strategic IT Plan'

PO2 Define the Information Architecture

Goal

Optimising the organisation of the development and maintenance of the information systems to satisfy the business requirements.

Activities

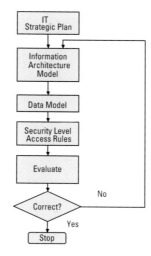

Figure 4.6 Activities of 'Define the Information Architecture'

The following activities are carried out in the IT process 'Define the Information Architecture':

- Create and regularly update an information architecture model
- Create and regularly update a corporate data dictionary which incorporates the organisation's data architecture
- Establish a general classification framework with regard to placement of data in information classes as well as allocation of ownership

- Define the access rules for the information classes
- Define, implement and maintain security levels for each of the data classifications identified above the level 'no protection required'
- Evaluate the information architecture model
- Monitor the process

Relationships with other processes

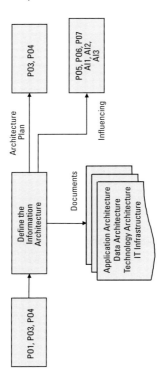

Figure 4.7 Relationships of 'Define the Information Architecture'

PO3 Determine Technological Direction

Goal

To take advantage of available and emerging technology to drive
and enable the business strategy.

Activities

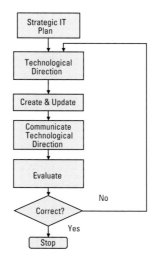

Figure 4.8 Activities of 'Determine Technological Direction'

The following activities are carried out in the IT process
'Determine Technological Direction':

- Create and regularly update a technology architecture plan
- Communicate the technological direction
- Continuously monitor the emerging IT trends
- Assess the capability of the infrastructure
- Define technology norms in order to speed up
  standardisation

- Evaluate the technological architecture plan
- Monitor the process

Relationships with other processes

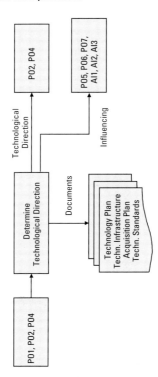

Figure 4.9 Relationships of 'Determine Technological Direction'

PO4   Define the IT Organisation and Relationships

Goal

To create an IT organisation to deliver the right IT services.

Activities

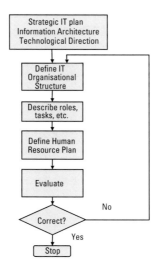

Figure 4.10 Activities of 'Define the IT Organisation and Relationships'

The following activities are carried out in the IT process 'Define the IT Organisation and Relationships':

- Organise IT at four levels: IT functions, IT department, IT director, IT Steering Committee (IT organisational structure)
- Describe roles, tasks, competence and responsibilities for all four levels
- Review of the organisational achievement
- Define staffing requirements

- Define the communications structure
- Define structure for ownership and custodianship
- Provide for supervision and duties segregation
- Define responsibility for physical and logical security
- Evaluate the IT organisation and relationships
- Monitor the process

Relationships with other processes

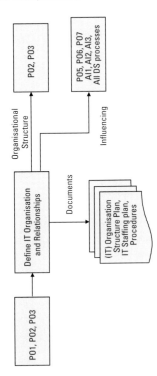

Figure 4.11 Relationships 'Define the IT Organisation and Relationships'

PO5   Manage the IT Investment

Goal

To ensure funding and to control disbursement of financial resources.

Activities

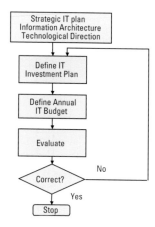

Figure 4.12 Activities of 'Manage the IT Investment'

The following activities are carried out in the IT process 'Manage the IT Investment':

- Define IT investment plan
- Define annual IT budgeting and controlling
- Arrange asset management
- Evaluate the annual IT budget
- Monitor the process

Relationships with other processes

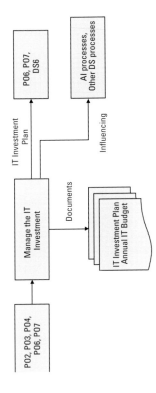

Figure 4.13   Relationships of 'Manage the IT Investment'

PO6   Communicate Management Aims and Direction

Goal

To ensure user awareness and understanding of management aims and direction.

Activities

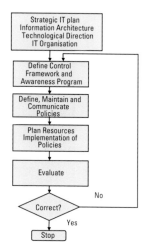

Figure 4.13 Activities of 'Communicate Management Aims and Direction'

The following activities are carried out in the IT process 'Communicate Management Aims and Direction':

- Create a framework and an awareness programme for a positive information control environment
- Define, develop, document and control policies covering general aims and directives
- Define the methods of communication
- Communicate the organisation policies

- Plan for appropriate resources for policy implementation
- Adjust policies to accommodate changing conditions
- Define, document and maintain the quality standards
- Develop and maintain a framework policy for security and internal control and communicating it to the organisation
- Provide and implement policy regarding intellectual property rights and other business integrity issues
- Evaluate the management aims and directions
- Monitor the process

Relationships with other processes

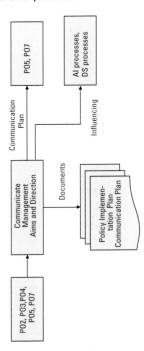

Figure 4.14 Relationships of 'Communicate Management Aims and Direction'

PO7   Manage Human Resources

Goal

Acquiring and maintaining a motivated and competent workforce
and maximising personnel contributions to the IT processes.

Activities

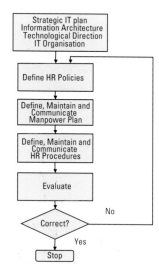

Figure 4.15 Activities of 'Manage Human Resources'

The following activities are carried out in the IT process 'Manage
Human Resources':

- Define human resources policies
- Formulate recruitment, promotion and termination policy
- Implement and regularly assess this policy
- Evaluate job performance
- Define the manpower required to support the service plan

- Consolidate manpower required for the project plan, service plan and career paths
- Identify existing and planned manpower
- Establish and evaluate alternative manpower plans
- Define education plan
- Document manpower and education plans
- Evaluate human resources policies
- Monitor the process

Relationships with other processes

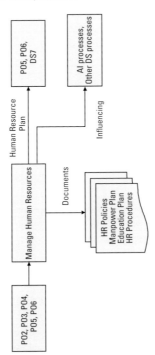

Figure 4.16 Relationships of 'Manage Human Resources'

PO8   Ensure compliance with External Requirements

Goal

Ensuring compliance with external requirements to meet legal, regulatory and contractual obligations.

Activities

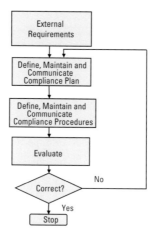

Figure 4.17 Activities of 'Ensure Compliance with External Requirements'

The following activities are carried out in the IT process 'Ensure Compliance with External Requirements':

- Define and maintain compliance plan
- Communicate compliance plan
- Define and maintain compliance procedures, rules and regulations
- Communicate compliance procedures, rules and regulations
- Monitor and evaluate compliance.

Relationships with other processes

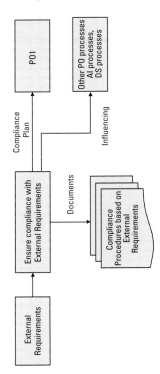

Figure 4.18   Relationships of 'Ensure Compliance with External Requirements'

PO9   Assess and Manage Risks

Goal

Assess risks to support management decisions through achieving
IT objectives and responding to threats by reducing complexity,
increasing objectivity and identifying important decision factors.

Activities

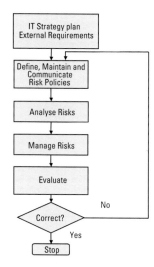

Figure 4.19 Activities of 'Assess and Manage Risks'

The following activities are carried out in the IT process 'Assess and
Manage Risks':

- Define and maintain risk policies
- Communicate risk policies
- Establish a risk assessment framework
- Establish a risk assessment approach
- Identify risks

- Assess risks
- Classify risks as: manageable, to be insured, to be contractually negotiated or self insured (risk analysis)
- Manage risks
- Define and implement a risk action plan
- Prioritise controls
- Evaluating risk policies and risks
- Monitor the process

Relationships with other processes

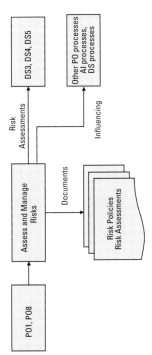

Figure 4.20 Relationships of 'Assess and Manage Risks'

PO10 Manage Projects

Goal

Manage projects to set priorities to start project activities to realise:

- Delivering project on time and within budget
- Improving earned value of projects
- Achieving the ROI of the projects (achieving project business and minimising costs)

Activities

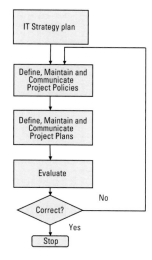

Figure 4.21 Activities of 'Manage Projects'

The following activities are carried out in the IT process 'Manage Projects':

- Define and maintain project policies
- Communicate project policies
- Define technically feasible and manageable projects

- Define project resources, time and service level requirements
  (including recovery, security and audit requirements)
- Define any unique control requirements for each project
- Communicate project plans
- Financially justify and prioritise the project plan
- Define service level planning
- Evaluate project policies and project plans
- Monitor the process

Relationships with other processes

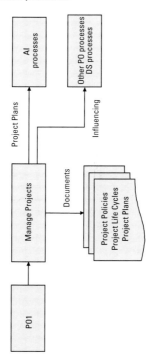

Figure 4.22 Relationships of 'Manage Projects'

PO11 Manage Quality

Goal

Manage quality to meet the customer requirements to reduce quality costs and to improve customer satisfaction.

Activities

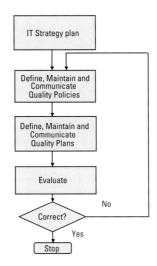

Figure 4.23 Activities of 'Manage Quality'

The following activities are carried out in the IT process 'Manage Quality':

- Define and maintain a general quality plan
- Define and maintain a quality assurance approach
- Select and implement methodology for the systems development lifecycle.
- Communicate the quality policy and quality plans
- Define and maintain the quality plans

- Define documentation standards
- Define testing and acceptance documentation standards
- Define quality metrics
- Report on quality assurance reviews
- Evaluate the quality policies and plans
- Monitor the process

Relationships with other processes

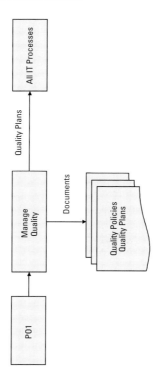

Figure 4.24 Relationships of 'Manage Quality'

AI   Acquisition and Implementation

AI1   Identify Automated Solutions

Goal

Identifying automated solutions to ensure an effective and efficient approach to satisfy the user requirements.

Activities

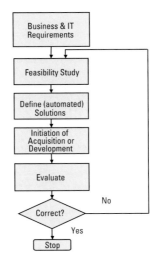

Figure 4.25 Activities of 'Identify Automated Solutions'

The following activities are carried out in the IT process 'Identify Automated Solutions':

- Define information requirements
- Formulate alternative courses of action
- Formulate acquisition strategy
- Define third-party service requirements

- Perform feasibility studies
- Design security controls and audit trails
- Select system software
- Acquire software product
- Contract application programming and software maintenance
- Evaluate identification of automated solutions
- Monitor the process

Relationships with other processes

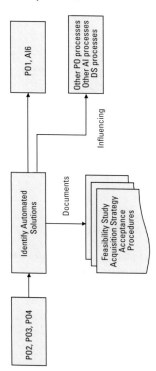

Figure 4.26 Relationships of 'Identify Automated Solutions'

AI2   Acquire and Maintain Application Software

Goal

Acquiring and maintaining application software to provide automated functions, which effectively support the business process.

Activities

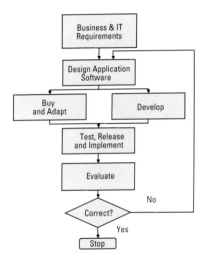

Figure 4.27 Activities of 'Acquire and Maintain Application Software'

The following activities are carried out in the IT process 'Acquire
and Maintain Application Software':

- Define and maintain application software policies
- Communicate application software policies
- Define and maintain application software documentation
- Define and maintain application software plans
- Communicate application software plans
- Define criteria for 'buy and adapt' and 'develop' application

software
- Define activities for application / software procurement and upgrade
- Define activities for maintenance
- Define plans for testing, releasing and implementation of application software
- Test application software
- Release application software
- Define activities for tuning and systems balancing
- Define activities for management system development and update
- Analyse differences between policies, plans and reality
- Define improvement actions
- Evaluate application software policies and plans
- Monitor the process

Relationships with other processes

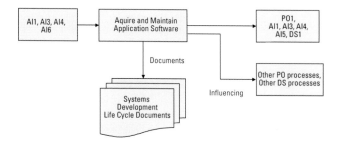

Figure 4.28 Relationships of 'Acquire and Maintain Application Software'

AI3   Acquire and Maintain Technology Infrastructure

Goal

Acquiring and maintaining technology infrastructure to provide the appropriate platforms to support business application requirements.

Activities

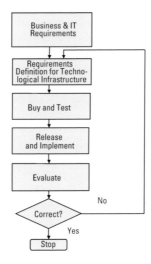

Figure 4.29 Activities of 'Acquire and Maintain Technology Infrastructure'

The following activities are carried out in the IT process 'Acquire and Maintain Technology Infrastructure':

- Define plans and requirements for technological infrastructure
- Assess new hardware and system software
- Acquire new hardware and system software
- Test new hardware and system software
- Implement new hardware and software

- Set-up preventative maintenance for hardware
- Evaluating the technological infrastructure
- Monitor the process

Relationships with other processes

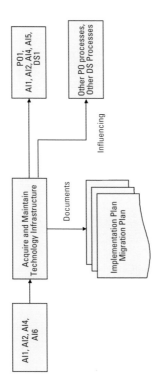

Figure 4.30 Relationships of 'Acquire and Maintain Technology Infrastructure'

AI4 Develop and Maintain Procedures

Goal

Developing and maintaining procedures to ensure the proper use of the applications and the technological solutions put in place.

Activities

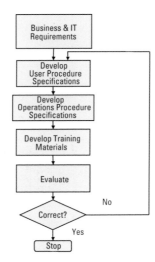

Figure 4.31 Activities of 'Develop and Maintain Procedures'

The following activities are carried out in the IT process 'Develop and Maintain Procedures':

- Develop User procedures manual
- Develop Operations manual
- Develop Training materials
- Evaluating procedures
- Monitor the process

Relationships with other processes

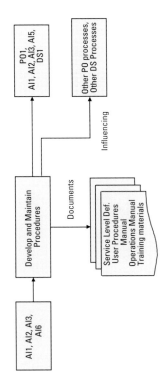

Figure 4.32 Relationships of 'Develop and Maintain Procedures'

AI5 Install and Accredit Systems

Goal

Installing and accrediting systems to verify and confirm that the solution is fit for the intended purpose.

Activities

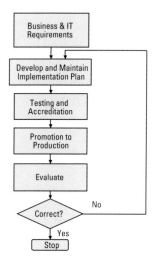

Figure 4.33 Activities of 'Install and Accredit Systems'

The following activities are carried out in the IT process 'Install and Accredit Systems':

- Develop and maintain implementation plan
- Provide training
- Define test plans and steps
- Functional testing
- Final acceptance testing
- Security testing and accreditation

- Operational testing
- Management's post-implementation review
- Evaluate implementation plan and accreditation process
- Monitor the process

Relationships with other processes

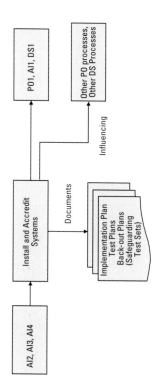

Figure 4.34   Relationships of 'Install and Accredit Systems'

AI6   Manage Changes

Goal

Managing changes to minimise the likelihood of disruption, unauthorised alterations, and errors.

Activities

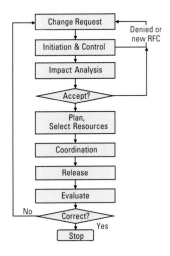

Figure 4.35 Activities of 'Manage Changes'

The following activities are carried out in the IT process 'Manage Changes':

- Change request initiation and control
- Impact assessment
- Authorise and accept changes
- Plan and control changes
- Select resources
- Assess documentation and procedures

- Co-ordinate release and distribution of software
- Close change
- Evaluate changes
- Monitor the process

Relationships with other processes

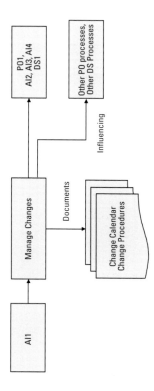

Figure 4.36 Relationships of 'Manage Changes'

DS   Delivery and Support

DS1   Define and Manage Service Levels

Goal

Defining and managing service levels to establish a common understanding of the level of service required.

Activities

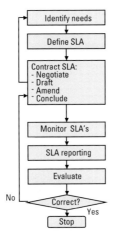

Figure 4.37 Activities of 'Define and Manage Service Levels'.
Source: IT Service Management, an introduction based on ITIL

The following activities are carried out in the IT process 'Define and Manage Service Levels':

- Identify service level requirements
- Define service level agreement framework
- Define service level agreements
- Manage service levels

- Monitor service levels
- Report service levels to customers
- Evaluate service level agreements and underpinning contracts
- Monitor the process

Relationships with other processes

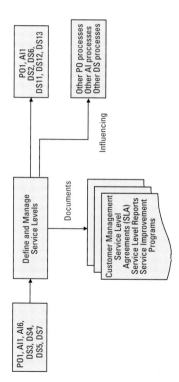

Figure 4.38 Relationships of 'Define and Manage Service Levels'

DS2   Manage Third-Party Services

Goal

Managing third-party services to ensure that roles and responsibilities of third parties are clearly defined, adhered to and continue to satisfy requirements.

Activities

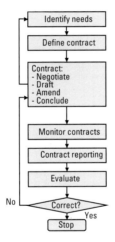

Figure 4.39 Activities of 'Manage Third-Party Services'

The following activities are carried out in the IT process 'Manage Third-Party Services':

- Identify third-party requirements
- Define service contracts
- Organise supplier interfaces
- Manage third-party and outsourcing contracts
- Monitor contract achievements
- Report service levels

- Evaluate third-party and outsourcing contracts
- Monitor the process

Relationships with other processes

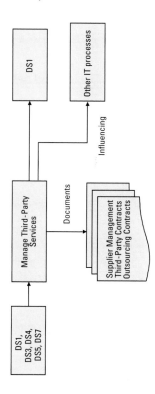

Figure 4.40 Relationships of 'Manage Third-Party Services'

DS3   Manage Performance and Capacity

Goal

Managing performance and capacity to ensure that adequate capacity is available and that best and optimal use is made of it to meet performance requirements.

Activities

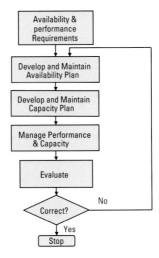

Figure 4.41 Activities of 'Manage Performance and Capacity'

The following activities are carried out in the IT process 'Manage Performance and Capacity':

- Define availability and performance requirements
- Develop availability plan
- Develop capacity plan
- Set up monitoring and reporting on availability and capacity
- Manage performance & capacity

- Evaluate performance and capacity
- Monitor the process

Relationships with other processes

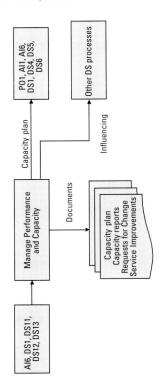

Figure 4.42 Relationships of 'Manage Performance and Capacity'

DS4   Ensure Continuous Service

Goal

Ensuring continuous service to make sure IT services are available as required and to ensure a minimum business impact in the event of a major disruption.

Activities

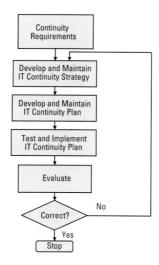

Figure 4.43 Activities of 'Ensure Continuous Service'

The following activities are carried out in the IT process 'Ensure Continuous Service':

- Define IT continuity requirements and strategy
- Carry out risk assessments
- Develop and maintain IT continuity plan
- Test and implement IT continuity plan
- Create and maintain recovery plans and procedures

- Educate and train users and managers
- Evaluate IT continuity plan and procedures
- Monitor the process

Relationships with other processes

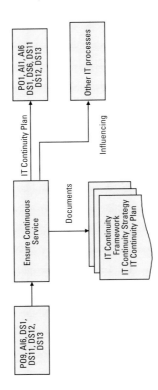

Figure 4.44   Relationships of 'Ensure Continuous Service'

DS5   Ensure Systems Security

Goal

Ensuring systems security to safeguard information against unauthorised use, disclosure or modification, damage or loss.

Activities

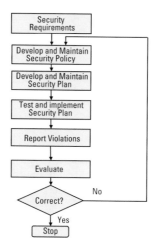

Figure 4.45 Activities of 'Ensure Systems Security'

The following activities are carried out in the IT process 'Ensure Systems Security':

- Define and manage systems security policy
- Define and maintain security measures and procedures
- Implement security measures and procedures
- Report security deviations and breaches of the rules and regulations
- Evaluate security policy, measures and procedures
- Monitor the process

Relationships with other processes

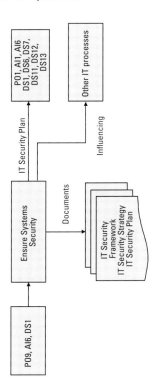

Figure 4.46 Relationships of 'Ensure Systems Security'

DS6   Identify and Allocate Costs

Goal

Identifying and allocating costs to ensure a correct awareness of
the costs attributable to IT services and to enable optimised
IT/Business decision making.

Activities

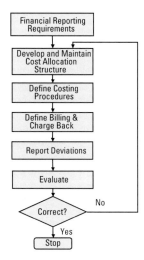

Figure 4.47 Activities of 'Identify and Allocate Costs'

The following activities are carried out in the IT process 'Identify
and Allocate Costs':

- Define and maintain cost allocation structure
- Identify chargeable items
- Define costing procedures
- Define user billing and charge back procedures
- Report deviations cost allocation structure

- Evaluate cost identification and cost allocation structure
- Monitor the process

Relationships with other processes

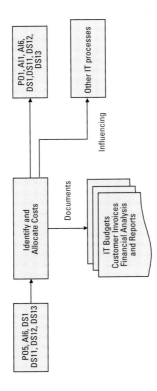

Figure 4.48 Relationships of 'Identify and Allocate Costs'

DS7   Educate and Train Users

Goal

Educating and training users to ensure that users are making effective use of technology and are aware of the risks and responsibilities involved.

Activities

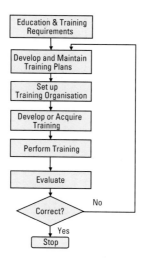

Figuree 4.49 Activities of 'Educate and Train Users'

The following activities are carried out in the IT process 'Educate and Train Users':

- Identify training needs/- requirements
- Develop and maintain training plan
- Set up training organisation
- Develop or acquire training
- Perform training

- Evaluate training
- Monitor the process

Relationships with other processes

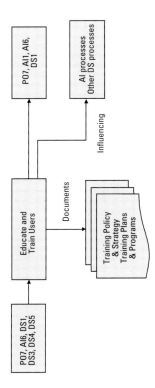

Figure 4.50 Relationships of 'Educate and Train Users'

DS8   Assist and Advise Customers

Goal

Assisting and advising customers to ensure that any problem experienced by the user is appropriately resolved.

Activities

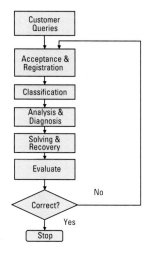

Figure 4.51 Activities of 'Assist and Advice Customers'

The following activities are carried out in the IT process 'Assist and Advice Customers':

- Registration of customer queries
- Acceptance of customer queries
- Classify customer queries
- Analysis and diagnosis
- Solving and recovery
- Customer query escalation

- Clearance of customer queries
- Evaluate customer advice and assistance
- Monitor the process

Relationships with other processes

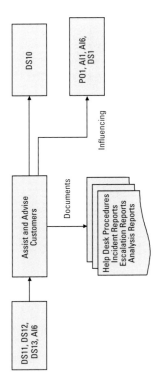

Figure 4.52 Relationships of 'Assist and Advice Customers'

DS9 Manage the Configuration

Goal

Managing the configuration to account for all IT components, prevent unauthorised alterations, verify physical existence and provide a basis for sound change management.

Activities

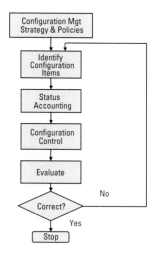

Figure 4.53 Activities of 'Manage the Configuration'

The following activities are carried out in the IT process 'Manage the Configuration':

- Define and maintain configuration management strategy, policies and procedures
- Configuration identification and recording
- Status accounting
- Configuration control

- Evaluate configuration management
- Monitor the process

Relationships with other processes

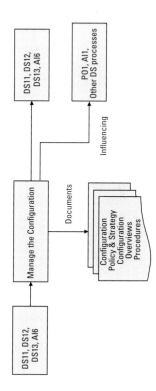

Figure 4.54 Relationships of 'Manage the Configuration'

DS10 Manage Problems and Incidents

Goal

Managing problems and incidents to ensure that problems and incidents are resolved and the cause is investigated to prevent any recurrence.

Activities

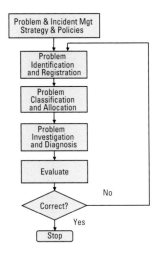

Figure 4.55 Activities of 'Manage Problems and Incidents'

The following activities are carried out in the IT process 'Manage Problems and Incidents':

- Define and maintain problem & incident management strategy and policies
- Problem & Incident identification and registration
- Problem & Incident classification and allocation
- Problem & Incident investigation and diagnosis

- Problem & Incident tracking and audit trail
- Evaluate Problem & Incident handling
- Monitor the process

Relationships with other processes

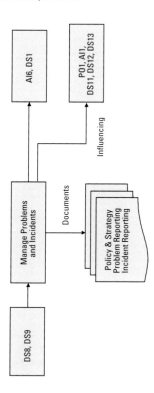

Figure 4.56   Relationships of 'Manage Problems and Incidents'

DS11 Manage Data

Goal

Managing data to ensure that data remains complete, accurate and valid during its input, update and storage.

Activities

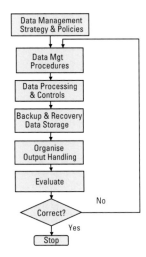

Figure 4.57 Activities of 'Manage Data'

The following activities are carried out in the IT process 'Manage Data':

- Develop and maintain data management strategy and policies
- Develop and monitor data acquisition procedures
- Develop and monitor data retention procedures
- Define and implement data processing and controls
- Ensure data integrity
- Define and implement backup & recovery of data storage

- Organise output handling
- Evaluate data management
- Monitor the process

Relationships with other processes

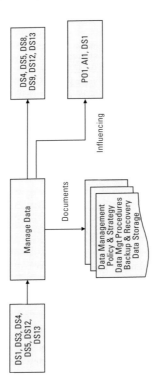

Figure 4.58   Relationships of 'Manage Data'

DS12 Manage Facilities

Goal

Managing facilities to provide suitable physical surroundings, which protects the IT equipment and people against man-made and natural hazards.

Activities

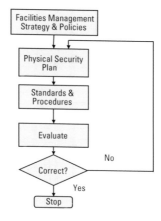

Figure 4.59 Activities of 'Manage Facilities'

The following activities are carried out in the IT process 'Manage Facilities':

* Develop and maintain facilities management strategy and procedures
* Define and implement physical security
* Define and implement standards and procedures
* Define access procedures
* Define personnel health and safety procedures
* Ensure availability measures

- Report facility management issues
- Evaluate facility management
- Monitor the process

Relationships with other processes

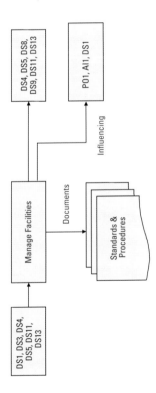

Figure 4.60 Relationships of 'Manage Facilities'

DS13 Manage Operations

Goal

Managing operations to ensure that important IT support functions are performed regularly and in an orderly fashion.

Activities

Figure 4.61 Activities of 'Manage Operations'

The following activities are carried out in the IT process 'Manage Operations':

- Develop and maintain operations strategy and policies
- Develop operations procedures and instructions
- Implement operations procedures and instructions
- Report controls for processing operations
- Monitor operations procedures and instructions
- Evaluate operations
- Monitor the process

Relationships with other processes

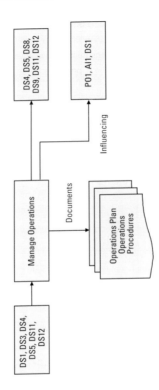

Figure 4.62 Relationships of 'Manage Operations'

M Monitoring

M1 Monitor the Processes

Goal

Monitor the processes to ensure the achievement of the performance objectives set for the IT processes.

Activities

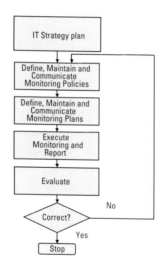

Figure 4.63 Activities of 'Monitor the Processes'

The following activities are carried out in the IT process 'Monitor the Processes':

- Define, maintain and communicate monitoring policies
- Define, maintain and communicate plans
- Collect monitoring data
- Assess performance

- Assess customer satisfaction
- Manage reporting for management
- Evaluate monitoring
- Monitor the process

Relationships with other processes

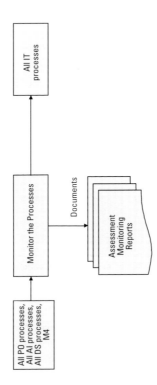

Figure 4.64 Relationships of 'Monitor the Processes'

M2   Assess Internal Control Adequacy

Goal

Assessing internal control adequacy to ensure the achievement of the internal control objectives set for the IT processes.

Activities

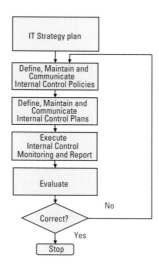

Figure 4.65 Activities of 'Assess Internal Control Adequacy'

The following activities are carried out in the IT process 'Assess Internal Control Adequacy':

- Define, maintain and communicate internal control policies
- Define, maintain and communicate internal control plans
- Define procedures for internal control
- Monitor internal controls
- Operate procedures for internal control
- Report internal control level

- Evaluate internal control adequacy
- Monitor the process

Relationships with other processes

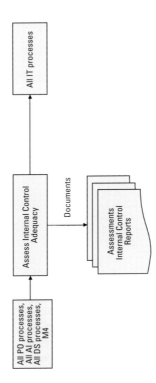

Figure 4.66 Relationships of 'Assess Internal Control Adequacy'

M3   Obtain Independent Assurance

Goal

Obtaining independent assurance to increase confidence and trust among the organisation, customers, and third-party providers.

Activities

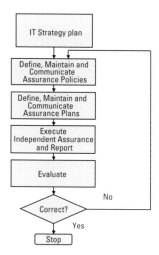

Figure 4.67 Activities of 'Obtain Independent Assurance'

The following activities are carried out in the IT process 'Obtain Independent Assurance':

- Define, maintain and communicate assurance policies
- Define, maintain and communicate assurance plans
- Contract independent assurance
- Accredit / certify security and internal control of IT services and third-party service providers
- Evaluate effectiveness of IT services and third-party service providers

- Assess compliance with laws and regulatory requirements and contractual commitments for internal IT organisation and third-party providers
- Evaluate independent assurance
- Monitor the process

Relationships with other processes

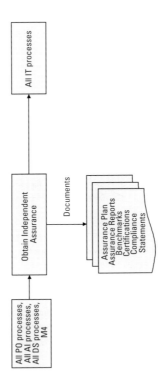

Figure 4.68   Relationships of 'Obtain Independent Assurance'

M4   Provide for Independent Audit

Goal

Providing for independent audit to increase confidence levels and benefit from best practice advice.

Activities

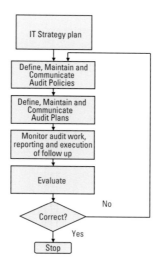

Figure 4.69 Activities of 'Provide for Independent Audit'

The following activities are carried out in the IT process 'Provide for Independent Audit':

- Define, maintain and communicate audit policies
- Define, maintain and communicate audit plans
- Develop audit charter
- Set up audit planning
- Monitor audit work
- Report audit results and execute follow-up activities

- Evaluate independence of audit work
- Monitor the process

Relationships with other processes

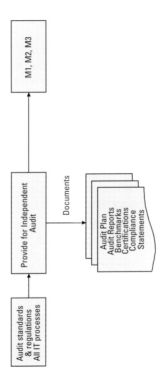

Figure 4.70 Relationships of 'Provide for Independent Audit'

Methods

Implementation of IT Governance within an organisation is a major effort, because organisational change is involved. Employees have to unlearn previous ways of working, move to a new way of working and become confident with it. This process has been described as the unfreeze - move - freeze cycle of change.

Implementation has to be managed as a project. Without any claim to completeness, the following project steps are required:

1. *Diagnosis*: Preparation and Situational Analysis
   - Define Stakeholders
2. *Model current situation*:
   - Process Analysis
   - Risk Analysis
   - Health Checks
3. *Strategy and Model desired situation and Gap Analysis*:
   - Maturity Model Evaluation
4. *Transition Strategy and Plan*:
   - Impact Analysis
   - Business Relevance
   - Project Plans
5. *Prepare for change* (per project):
   - Create customised metrics, guidelines, work programmes
   - Assign responsibilities
   - Create awareness
   - Train people
   - Define Self-Assessments
   - Implement Process Monitoring & Evaluation
   - Communication about Project Status Reports
6. *Monitor & Evaluate project*:
   - Define Project Metrics

In every project not only the tasks performed and the deliverables produced have to be taken into consideration, but also the communication and cultural context (preconceptions, values and attitudes).

Available tools

A number of tools are included in COBIT:

- The *Implementation Tool Set* contains the Diagnostics and Self-assessments.
- The *Management Guidelines* contains Maturity Measurements based on CMM, Performance Metrics and Critical Success Factors.
- IT Governance Implementation Guide Using COBIT.

COBIT Management Advisor, a commercial product of Methodware, contains a database of Critical Success Factors, Key Goal Indicators, Key Performance Indicators, and Maturity Steps for each of COBIT's 34 IT processes. The product enables companies to assess an IT process and provides better assurance that key IT risks are being identified and managed. Royal Philips Electronics developed the Process Service Tool as an internal benchmark for measuring the maturity of their IT-processes. This benchmark is based on more than 150 sites.

Another available product is EZCOBIT[2]. This product is available free via the InfosecAfrica website. This tool can help you to investigate the status of your company's IT processes compared to COBIT.

Several companies are currently working on Implementation Tools for IT-processes, based on COBIT. Other companies are working on models for health check and awareness, extending the maturity measurement to the business processes (first step for Corporate Governance).

2) This product is not endorsed or sponsored by ISACA/ITGI.

ISACA offers a one-hour presentation with an overview of CoBiT. This course is offered free of cost to ISACA chapters as a mini-PSS (Professional Seminar Series program) course. ISACA also offers a one day course to explore the CoBiT Summary, Framework, Detailed Control Objectives, Audit Guidelines and Management Guidelines. In addition ISACA offers a 'CoBiT Implementation Course' which presents the steps for structured implementation of CoBiT. The latter course delivers a general guideline as an aid for implementing CoBiT in particular organisations.

ITGI is developing a CoBiT Basic level e-learning course, and a revised course for Assurance professionals which will be available in early 2005.

Apart from ISACA, trainers all over the world offer CoBiT based courses that are developed from personal experience. In the near future more products for training and certification are expected.

The following table contains an explanation of terminology and acronyms used in this pocket guide.

Availability	The extent to which a system or service is available to the intended users at the required times
BNQP	Baldridge National Quality Program
BS7799	British Standard on Information Security Management
BSC	Balanced Scorecard
CIMA	Chartered Institute of Management Accountants
CIPE	Center for International Private Enterprise
CISA	Certified Information Systems Auditor
CoBiT	Control Objectives for Information and related Technology
CMM	Capability Maturity Model
CMMI	Capability Maturity Model Integration
Compliance	The extent to which processes act in accordance with those laws, regulations and contractual arrangements to which the process is subject
Confidentiality	The extent to which data is only accessible to a well-defined group of authorised persons
Control	The policies, procedures, practices and organisational structures designed to provide reasonable assurance that business objectives will be achieved and that undesired events will be prevented or detected and corrected
Corporate Governance	Is the system by which business corporations are directed and controlled. The Corporate Governance structure specifies the distribution of rights and responsibilities among different par-

	ticipants in the corporation, such as the board, managers, shareholders and other stakeholders, and spells out the rules and procedures for making decisions on corporate affairs. By doing this, it also provides the structure through which the company objectives are set, and the means of attaining those objectives and monitoring performance (OECD)
COSO	Committee of Sponsoring Organisations of the Treadway Commission
Effectiveness	The extent to which the information serves the defined objectives
Efficiency	The extent to which activities with regard to the provision of information are carried out at an acceptable cost and effort
EFQM	European Foundation for Quality Management
ERM	Enterprise Risk Management
IIA	Institute of Internal Auditors
Integrity	The extent to which data corresponds with the actual situation represented by that data
ISACA	Information Systems Audit and Control Association
ISACF	Information Systems Audit and Control Foundation
ISO	International Organisation for Standardisation
ISO/IEC 15408	Evaluation Criteria for Information Technology Security (Common Criteria). An International Standard on IT Security
ISO/IEC 15504	International Standard on Assessment Methods based on SPICE

ISO/IEC 17799	International Standard on Information Security Management
ISO9000	Quality management and quality assurance standards as defined by ISO
IT Control Objective	A statement of the desired result or purpose to be achieved by implementing control procedures in a particular IT activity
IT Governance	Is the system by which IT within enterprises is directed and controlled. The IT Governance structure specifies the distribution of rights and responsibilities among different participants, such as the board, business and IT managers, and spells out the rules and procedures for making decisions on IT. By doing this, it also provides the structure through which the IT objectives are set, and the means of attaining those objectives and monitoring performance
IT Governance (COBIT)	A structure of relationships and processes to direct and control the enterprise in order to achieve the enterprise's goals by adding value while balancing risk versus return over IT and its processes
ITGI	IT Governance Institute
IT Resource - Application Systems	The sum of manual and programmed procedures
IT Resource - Data	The representation of relevant external and internal objects. Structured and non-structured, graphics, sound, etc
IT Resource - Facilities	The resources to house and support business and information systems

IT Resource - People	The human resources needed to plan, organise, acquire, deliver, support and monitor information systems and services
Technical Infrastructure	Covers hardware, operating systems, database management systems, networking software etc.
ITIL	Information Technology Infrastructure Library
ITSMF	IT Service Management Forum
MOF	Microsoft Operations Framework
OECD	Organisation for Economic Co-operation and Development
OGC	UK Office of Government Commerce
PDCA-cycle	Plan-do-check-act cycle developed by Deming
Reliability of Information	Relates to the provision of appropriate information for management to operate the entity and for management to exercise its financial and compliance reporting responsibilities
SPICE	Software Process Improvement and Capability Determination-an initiative on software process improvement
TOE	Target of Evaluation
SEI	Software Engineering Institute of the Carnegie Mellon University

Literary sources

Bon, Jan van (ed.). *IT Service Management, an introduction based on ITIL*. ITSMF, 2002

Bon, Jan van (ed.). *Compendium IT Service Management*. Web document at http://en.itsmportal.net/goto/literatuur/boek/118.xml.

CIMA. *Enterprise Governance - A CIMA discussion paper*, www.cimaglobal.com, 2004.

CIPE. *Instituting Corporate Governance in developing, emerging and transitional economies: A Handbook.* Center for International Private Enterprise, March 2002.

COSO. *Internal Control - Integrated Framework (COSO report).* Committee of Sponsoring Organizations of the Treadway Commission, 1994.

Grembergen, Wim van, Ph.D. *The IT Balanced Scorecard and IT Governance.* ITGI, 2001.

Haazen, Walter. *Choosing your IT-Scorecard Framework.* ASP.Consulting Group, 2002.

Hamaker, Stacey, CISA, "Spotlight on Governance". In: *Information Systems Control Journal*®, Volume 1, 2003

Hopstaken, B. & A. Kranendonk. *Informatiebeleid; puzzelen met beleid en plan.* Kluwer 1996.

CobiT sources

The following publications were released by the CobiT Steering
Committee and the IT Governance Institute:

CobiT *3rd Edition, Executive Summary.* ISACF, July 2000

CobiT *3rd Edition, Framework.* ISACF, July 2000

CobiT *3rd Edition, Control Objectives.* ISACF, July 2000,

CobiT *3rd Edition, Management Guidelines.* ISACF, July 2000

CobiT *3rd Edition, Audit Guidelines.* ISACF, July 2000

CobiT *3rd Edition, Implementation Tool Set.* ISACF, July 2000

Board Briefing on IT Governance, 2nd Edition. ITGI, 2003

*Information Security Governance, Guidance for Boards of Directors
and Executive Management.* ISACF, 2001

IT Governance Executive Summary. ITGI, 2002

IT Strategy Committee. ITGI, 2002

IT Control Practice Statements. ITGI, 2002

Web sources

A limited number of references is provided.

ISACA	www.isaca.org
IT Governance Institute Portal	www.itgi.org
EZCOBIT	www.cobit.co.za
Balanced Scorecard	www.balancedscorecard.org
CMM	http://www.sei.cmu.edu/cmm
CMMI	http://www.sei.cmu.edu/cmmi/

The IT Governance Portal contains an extensive links page for use by the audience to this book.